# William of Orange

# The Silent Prince

# William of Orange

# The Silent Prince

by

## W.G. Van de Hulst

**INHERITANCE PUBLICATIONS**
**NEERLANDIA, ALBERTA, CANADA**
**PELLA, IOWA, U.S.A.**

**Canadian Cataloguing in Publication Data**

Hulst, W. G. van de (Willem Gerrit), 1879 - 1963
   William of Orange, the silent prince

   translation of: Willem van Oranje, vader des vaderlands
   ISBN 0-921100-15-9

   1. William I, Prince of Orange, 1533-1584—Juvenile literature.
I. Title
DH188.W7H8413 1992   j949.2'03'092   C92-091635-7

**Library of Congress Cataloguing-in-Publication Data**

Hulst, W. G. van de (Willem Gerrit), 1879-1963
   [Willem van Oranje, vader des vaderlands. English]
   William of Orange, the silent prince / by W.G. Van de Hulst.
      p.   cm.
   Translation of: Willem van Oranje, vader des vaderlands.
   ISBN 0-921100-15-9 (pbk.)
   1. William I, Prince of Orange, 1533-1584—Juvenile literature.
2. Netherlands—Kings and rulers—Biography—Juvenile literature.
I. Title.
DH188.W7H813  1992
949.2'03'092—dc20
[B]                                                            92-20246
                                                                   CIP
                                                                    AC

Translated from the Dutch by Alice Veenendaal
Published in English with permission from J.N. Voorhoeve, Den Haag, The Nether-
lands
Illustrations by W.G. Van de Hulst, Jr.
Cover illustration by H. Sturris

ISBN 0-921100-15-9

3rd Printing 2000

Published simultaneously in the United Kingdom by
Inheritance Publications (U.K.) 19 Tench Way, Romsey, Hants, SO51 7RX

Published simultaneously in U.S.A. by Inheritance Publications
Box 366, Pella, Iowa  50219

Available in Australia from Inheritance Publications
Box 1122, Kelmscott, W.A. 6111  Tel. & Fax (089) 390 4940

Printed in Canada

# Contents

# 1. My Son

Hush! He was asleep. Snuggled deep under the soft satin blankets in the beautiful cradle, he slept, safe and secure.

Deep in slumber, the tiny mouth quivered. A smile trembled briefly. Was he dreaming? What of? Who could say? All little children have dreams, the poor farmer's son as well as the wealthy son in his satin bed. Perhaps their dreams are the same.

It was quiet in the room. Golden rays of evening sunshine streamed through the little diamond panes of the tall, narrow windows. It was the hour for little ones to sleep.

Stained glass figures of the royal coat of arms decorated the windows. Sunshine set the colours ablaze, casting their jewelled reflections on the polished, wood floor.

Slowly, cautiously, the door opened. A woman looked in. She tilted her head, listening. Was he sleeping? Her friendly countenance creased into a smile. On tiptoe she approached the cradle. Briefly she hesitated, then pushed the satin curtain aside.

There he lay. His dark curls shone in the golden light. Her son. She bent down and softly kissed the round, flushed cheek.

How could such a small, sleeping child know that his mother had kissed him? And how could such a child know the depth of his mother's love? Whether a poor farmer's son in his cradle of wood or a wealthy boy in a bed of satin — in this they were equal.

"My son!"

His mother smiled. But then, gradually, her kindly face grew sober, and her eyes clouded with uncertainty. Her son! Now he slept in his warm bed in this inner chamber of the castle, secure and protected. Now they could care for him and watch over him. But soon he would grow up to be strong and independent. The world was so big, so vast, so full of danger . . . and so cruel . . .

Would he be a good man, a faithful knight, a true nobleman? Would he be handsome, honest, God-fearing? Would his life be full of happiness and success? Or would he become a miscreant? Oh, it was possible! The poor mother shuddered. She did not know what the future held for him. Only God knew.

Then, beside the beautiful cradle, above the small, sleeping head, the mother folded her hands in prayer for her little son. What would she pray? What should she ask of the heavenly Father whose will guided the lives of all people? Should she plead for riches or wisdom or for a long, happy life? Should she ask that he be a brave man feared by his enemies? Should she pray that he become famous so that all men would speak well of him? Or should she just ask for all things good and pure, all things wonderful for her beloved son?

No! This mother was a devout woman. She knew very well that the good and wonderful things of this world were

JULIANA·GRAVIN·VAN·STOLBERG

*Juliana of Stolberg 1506 - 1580*

fleeting. They would not bring true happiness. No, she would not ask for such things. She prayed just one request: that God would care for him and keep him as His child forever.

The Lord knew what was best for her son far better than she did. And so she surrendered him to God's sacred keeping and was content. The smile returned. Yes, this young life could be blessed with happiness and prosperity. There would also be difficulty, grief, and pain, but in God's fatherly arms her son would be safe. So let joy or sorrow, glory or suffering, come. She would help to bear them.

Juliana of Stolberg, loving and God-fearing mother, carefully closed the door. William slept peacefully.

The setting sun sank beneath the horizon. The jewelled figures on the gleaming floor faded away. Twilight fell. It was night.

\*       \*       \*

Deep in the heart of Germany lay the earldom of Nassau. Dillenburg was the count's castle. With its towers and gardens surrounded by thick, strong walls, it sat high on the mountainside, its mighty drawbridge spanning the tumultuous Dille River. In those days, many of the noble dwellings were situated in similar settings. The castle was isolated, surrounded by dense woods and vast, rolling plains.

Count William of Nassau was the master of this stronghold as well as lord over the villages and towns scattered around the countryside. Juliana of Stolberg was his wife. The little one tucked in his cradle of satin was their firstborn, the son who bore his father's name, William of Nassau. Eventually he would succeed his father, inherit the estate, and rule in his stead. Someday . . . But that day was in the future — unknown and unrevealed. Through the years, more sons were born in the great castle. They were John, Louis, Adolphus, Henry. Seven daughters were also born. Their mother filled their lives with fun and happiness. Her eldest son, her firstborn, was loved and cherished along with the others — perhaps a little more.

## 2. The Lowlands by the Sea

It was evening. A young boy roamed the battlements of the castle, Dillenburg. He was eleven years old. His younger brothers and sisters and his fellow companions with whom he studied and played remained inside. The sun had descended toward the horizon. Soon it would be time to go to bed. He had wandered through the great halls of the castle and then slipped outside, up onto the battlements. There, one had a splendid view of the great, wide world.

Dillenburg rested upon a rocky mount in much the same way as a crown sat upon a king's head. As far as the eye could see, the green, fertile land, the rolling hills and winding rivers, the villages and market towns all belonged to Dillenburg. Count William of Nassau was master of this beautiful land. The boy who wandered about the castle battlements on this calm evening was also named William of Nassau. He was his father's eldest son — and heir. Someday, after his father had died, he would be master. Someday, after he had grown up.

His elbows resting on the rough, stone wall, his chin propped in his hands, he gazed into the distance, westward to where the towering clouds formed a golden archway above the fireball of the setting sun. What a splendid sight!

What had drawn the boy to the solitude of the castle heights, away from the companionship of his playmates? Was he shy or moody? Not at all! Life in Dillenburg was pleasant, full of merriment. William was a happy, jolly lad, full of energy and fun. Each day he attended school. Various talented tutors gave lessons to the children of Count William of Nassau and Juliana of Stolberg and to the children of noble families living in the area. The boys and girls lived, studied, and played together in the great castle. The castle-school was of good repute, and the good lady of the castle who cared for the children as a mother was greatly respected. It was an honour for the noblemen to entrust their children to her.

Shy and moody? Not the prince! He was as happy and fun-loving as his friends, but he also thoroughly enjoyed his lessons, especially those that were the most difficult and challenging. He was very intelligent and enjoyed sports and games. Riding, fencing, shooting, swimming, racing — all were performed with great zeal. His heart burned to become a brave, strong, noble knight.

Tonight, on this beautiful evening, he gazed into the golden distance. Never had he ventured so far into the world. He had accompanied his father or one of his tutors on horseback or on foot throughout the nearby woodlands and fields. But there in the West where the sun sank below the horizon lay the lowlands beside the sea: Holland, Zealand, Flanders, and others. There lay vast stretches of field and water but no hills or mountains. They must be wonderful lands! He had learned much about them but had never seen them. Would he ever?

Of course, once he had grown up, he would go on long journeys to far-off places. But naturally he would always return home to Dillenburg. This was his father's castle. Here he would rule. And then? Yes, then what? Well, then he would be a good count, like his father. Then he would care for all the people on his lands, faithfully and justly, as his father did now.

Suddenly, as he gazed and dreamed, he was startled to see a cloud of dust drifting above the road. Just before they disappeared behind the trees and houses of the village, he recognized a party of horsemen. Then, as they reappeared, he could clearly see they were but a small cavalcade of four or five, perhaps six, riders. Maybe they were coming to the castle. It was possible, for horsemen often stopped here. They never presented a problem, for the castle was large, and the spacious stables could house more than a hundred horses.

William's mother always welcomed guests. Dillenburg was well known for its hospitality, and William resolved that later, when he was master, this would also be the case.

"Hospitality, cordiality, and kindness are virtuous qualities," his mother quoted.

Of course princes, counts, kings, and even emperors were to be virtuous, noble men.

William had forgotten the approaching riders. Soon the clock would chime and it would be bedtime. Then Mother would come to his room. This was always the best part of the day, for then, for a little while, she would pause in her busy life and belong only to him. Mother . . .

He sprinted down the stone steps and headed for the wing where the sleeping quarters were located. Far below, hooves clattered over the wooden drawbridge which crossed the swiftly flowing mountain river, the Dille.

## 3. Father and Mother

Later that evening, two people sat together in the great hall of Dillenburg. They were William of Nassau and his wife, Juliana of Stolberg. Their hearts were troubled over their eldest son, William. They were confused. Their feelings were a jumble of joy, anxiety, and distress mingled with a general sense of uneasiness and even a certain amount of pride. Yes, they were very proud of their son, and yet their joy was clouded with anxiety and deep sorrow.

This very evening a party of horsemen arrived at the castle just before the drawbridge had been raised for the night. Their unexpected visit and message caused the conflicting emotions in the hearts of William's parents. Young William was the reason for their coming, although he was unaware of it when he watched their dusty approach earlier that evening. Even now he knew nothing. His sleep was peaceful.

Their mission was of utmost importance. They brought a message that the boy would never be able to guess, much less dream of. It was a message that would completely change his life — that same future he had envisioned while contemplating his father's lands in the golden glow of the setting sun.

William must leave his home. Why? Because the emperor wanted him to do so. The horsemen were important men, ambassadors of the great and powerful emperor, Charles V. They had come bearing riches, power, and honour for young William. Rene of Chalons, William's cousin, had died in battle. He had died childless, and now William, as the eldest son of the count of Nassau, was his heir. Rene of Chalons had been the prince of Orange, a small, rich principality in far-off France. Now young William had become the prince of Orange, and all Rene's wealth and possessions belonged to him. This was certainly cause for joy. But the messengers had brought more news. This young boy, suddenly an important prince, could no longer live at Dillenburg, a remote castle in German territory.[1] His new position required him to live at the imperial palace with the emperor in Brussels. Emperor Charles V, the most powerful ruler in the world, wanted William to live with him, wanted to care for him, wanted to treat him as his own child. That should certainly make his parents very proud. Certainly they had every reason for joy and pride, and yet . . .

There they sat together in the great hall. The distinguished visitors had already retired for the night. They had delivered their happy news. But Count William and his wife could not sleep. Their hearts were too full of joy and disquiet. Their eldest son was to leave them and Dillenburg to live in far-away Brussels. That was a serious matter, and yet it was not the worst. There was more to burden their hearts.

The emperor's palace was full of wealth and magnificence, but it was full of iniquity too. Who would pray with the young boy as his mother did now? Who would guide him in the godly way? Who would teach him that the things of eternity were of far greater value than all the splendour and glory of this earthly life? Would not young William forget God in such a place?

Father and Mother were no longer Roman Catholics. Luther, the great reformer, who in 1517 had nailed his Ninety-five Theses on the door of the Wittenberg chapel, had deeply stirred their hearts. Count William of Nassau, as a prince of Germany, had attended the Diet of Worms.[2] Martin Luther had been called upon to defend his faith before the mighty Emperor

---

[1] The realm of Orange no longer exists. In 1713, under the rule of Louis XIV, Orange became a province of France.

[2] The Diet of Worms had taken place in 1521, twenty-three years earlier.

Charles and all the eminent cardinals and bishops of the Roman Catholic church. There Luther had spoken those unforgettable words, "Here I stand, I cannot do otherwise. So help me God." Count William had heard those words and had been deeply moved. Later, he and Juliana became followers of Luther. Their son William followed in their footsteps. But in Brussels, in the imperial palace, everyone followed the Roman beliefs. There William would attend the Roman Catholic church. Perhaps he would forget everything his parents had taught him. This was the fear, the intense grief that overshadowed the joy in the honour bestowed on their child.

However, the emperor's wish must be obeyed. Juliana bowed her head. She remembered the evening so long ago when her son had lain in his cradle, when peace had filled her heart. Even now the Lord knew what was best for him better than she did. And so, once again, she entrusted him into God's sacred keeping. There he would be safe. Dillenburg would be quieter without his rowdiness. There would be one less to care for and watch over, but there would not be one less to pray for. William would need the prayers of his mother. Tomorrow she would tell William.

## 4. The Emperor's Favourite

Brussels, capital city of the United Netherlands, the seventeen provinces, which were united for the first time under the rule of the mighty Emperor Charles V.

Brussels was the richest, most beautiful city in the country. Here stood the imperial palace where Mary of Hungary, the emperor's sister, ruled as governess.

Brussels was also the city of tournaments and the city of pomp and splendour to the nobility and knights who lived near and in the imperial court.

In the centre of the city, not far from the imperial palace, stood another beautiful castle. Sentries stood guard on the stone steps leading to its entrance. More guards were posted at the outer gate.

The massive doors swung open. A youth, elegantly dressed in velvet and silk wearing a beret with waving plumes upon his head, stepped over the threshold. The guards raised

their spears and stood at attention, rigid as statues in respectful salute. Quickly returning their greeting, the youth hurried down the steps to the forecourt, where horses stood in readiness. The magnificent animals restlessly pawed and pranced but were held in check by grooms clad in royal livery. The splendid gray horse was his. Springing into the saddle, he quickly brought the spirited animal under control. He had a masterful hand and was a capable horseman. The men who followed him also mounted their horses, and the lively, colourful procession rode through the gates into the narrow city streets. The princely youth led the way. Their destination was the imperial palace. Although the palace was nearby, such an important nobleman, the squire of the emperor, could not simply walk about the streets like a common delivery boy. He must ride forth with a retinue befitting his princely position.

Those watching the procession greeted the riders respectfully and smiled. The people of Brussels recognized this squire of the emperor, and everyone was familiar with his friendly manner. He was well liked. If someone wondered and questioned the identity of the youth who lived in the beautiful castle and rode forth as a young prince, then others would answer in amazement, "Don't you know who that is? Doesn't everyone in Brussels know the young prince of Orange, the emperor's favourite?"

The emperor was in the city now. These were happy times for William. The emperor loved him, but, then, William loved the emperor too. Not only did he love him but he honoured his imperial master with all the ardour and loyalty of his youthful heart.

The mighty emperor, though his life was grand, was bothered and worried. His gaze was sombre; he looked much older than he actually was. Yet William could make him laugh when he entered his room and doffed his beret as he knelt on one knee.

"Come forward, Prince!"

He spoke Dutch, yet the young prince understood him. If the emperor would ask a question in French, then William would reply in French. He was clever and studied with diligence. His tutor, Perot, had been chosen by the emperor. Time and again when the emperor inquired concerning William's progress, the answer was, "Excellent, your majesty. He will become one of your most competent attendants."

William was also a sensible, thoughtful boy. He was not one who simply memorized lessons and mechanically repeated what he had learned. William remembered what he studied, thought it over, and used his knowledge. He did not chatter mindlessly. He thought before he spoke. It was just that quality that endeared him to the wise emperor.

William assumed his position behind the emperor's throne as was fitting for a page. There were many important men present. They were some of the most prominent men in the country. Others were trusted ambassadors representing their masters. Kindly, the emperor addressed them all. At his nod, conversation stopped. Important matters needed to be discussed with the ambassadors of a foreign prince. Only the most trusted of the emperor's advisors were allowed to remain in the room.

Others were not permitted to listen to the secret affairs of state. But what about the young page? He prepared to leave as well. But the emperor nodded. William must stay. The foreign ambassadors were astonished. He could so easily betray secrets.

But the emperor smiled and said, "William of Orange is my trustworthy confidant." And he thought to himself, someday he will be my trustworthy advisor. He will not disappoint me; he has a heart of gold.

Yes, William would stay. His dark eyes glowed, and his heart swelled with pride. It was wonderful to be trusted like this. Would he disclose secrets, betray the confidence of his emperor? Never. He would listen carefully and betray nothing. Silently he promised, my master, my good master, I honour you with all my heart. I will always be true to you. I promise to serve you with all my might. I am yours.

And so as William stood motionless behind his master, his eyes shining, he was more proud than a knight in a glorious tournament.

When the ambassadors left, William received some pleasant news. The emperor planned to tour Germany. He would be accompanied by his important knights, a number of servants, and a strong body of horsemen. William was to go too, as the emperor's page! That was an honour indeed. Cheering crowds and waving banners would welcome them in every town and village. In the imperial cortege, William would ride directly behind his master. The emperor was to discuss many matters of importance with the German leaders. William would be there. He would attend his master as his confidant, as his young friend, yes, even as his own son. What greater pleasure was there?

## 5. Sickening Smoke

William of Orange grew up to be a fine nobleman. His life was full and rich, a continuous round of splendid events. In his own palace he was a great ruler surrounded by hundreds of servants ready to obey his every command. But such a privileged life did not make him proud or boastful. Men liked the happy, sensible, young prince who treated nobility and common citizens with friendly courtesy. He was a capable horseman and handled his weapons with speed and skill. Prince William looked forward to a bright future filled with happiness and prosperity. Already he was the emperor's friend. Later he would become his advisor. Eventually, the Prince of Orange would hold the highest position in the government of the country. He was worthy of it. Everyone acknowledged that.

But there was also another member of the imperial household who would rise to great power, who would hold a position more important. In fact, he would be lord and master of the Prince of Orange. He was Philip, the emperor's son.

Philip was a strange man, quiet and withdrawn. He was not adept at studying, horsemanship, or combat. He did not view the world with openness and honesty. He was proud and arrogant. He did not trust others, for his own heart was not honest. Philip had no affection for the young Prince of Orange. Instead, he begrudged the love and affection the people had for William. Even more, he resented the friendship extended by his imperial father to the young prince. However, he was very careful to disguise his feelings. They were cunningly concealed in his heart.

The Prince of Orange was happy and content. Life was good. But then he had never been one to mope or complain. Faithfully he attended the Roman Catholic church. Even there he had a place of honour. At the front of the church stood the splendid chairs reserved for the governess, Mary, and her distinguished courtiers. William sat there too, with a velvet covered prayer stool at his feet. There at the front of the beautiful cathedral they sat, close to the altars, close to the holy statues, close to the priests. Did they also sit close to God?

At home with his mother at Dillenburg, it had been different — perhaps not as splendid, but it had seemed more genuine, more honest. Here it seemed as though men had left their hearts at home and prayed only with their lips. His mother had taught him otherwise. But while he was here, he must never let his thoughts dwell on his former home or the way in which they had worshipped. That would be a grave mistake. The Bible, translated by Luther into German, was a forbidden book. His teachers had made that clear to him, and the priests had warned him about reading it. William would have to become completely Roman Catholic if he wished to be a good and faithful servant of the emperor. All who did not revere and respect the holy Roman church, the provider of salvation, were despised by him. Would the emperor not hate William if he did not forget the faith of his former home, the faith of his father and mother? These thoughts bothered him; his heart ached.

But then he was young and strong. Life was so much fun, so busy, so wonderful. Heaven was still so far away. Why should he be so worried about religion? Perhaps later. Why did men argue so bitterly about the worship of God? It was absurd. He desired to be a knight, free of fear or reproach, counselor to the emperor, leader of the imperial soldiers, a national hero. He also wanted to be a pious son of the Roman Catholic church. What was the difference to him? And yet . . .

Sometimes a foul reek of burning wood and flesh pervaded the narrow streets of Brussels. Then a dark cloud of thick, smoky smog blocked the light of the sun until the wind dispersed it. But in the meantime someone, a human being, had been strangled, then bound to a stake and placed above a pile

of burning fagots. Sometimes jeering crowds pressed and jostled together behind the executioner's men, men dressed in black, wearing black masks which hid all but the sinister cruelty that glittered in their eyes. They followed the priest, who bore the holy crucifix at the head of the procession. In the eyes of the people and in the grim expressions of their faces there lurked fear mingled with anger and hatred. A fellow human was burning. Why, oh why, must this happen? Why must a man or woman die? Were those who died in the flames nothing but common criminals?

In Brussels, the young Prince of Orange, caught up in the pleasures of his carefree, happy life also saw the thick, dark clouds rising from the burning pyres to blot out the sun's light. He saw the grim faces of the people and heard their heartless cheers. Into his merry heart crept doubt and disquiet. Why did the men and women who refused to listen to the Roman Catholic priests and their teachings concerning God and heaven need to be captured, tortured, and killed? Surely they were not criminals guilty of serious crimes. Had they sinned so terribly? What then of William's own father who allowed the new teachings in his own country? And what of his devout mother? And why did the persecuted bear the dreadful pain of torture, of death, so patiently, so faithfully? That could only be possible if they firmly believed themselves to be children of God. Yet they served and worshipped the Lord in such a different way from what the priests allowed.

Compassion for those oppressed people stirred in William's heart. He could not believe it was such a grave sin to be a "heretic."[1] The emperor would not tolerate heresy. He wanted one empire, one people, one religion. Those who dared

---

[1] A heretic is someone who confesses a heretical (wrong, unbiblical) doctrine. The Roman Catholics condemned the Reformed people as heretics and for many years they were commonly called by that name. It speaks for itself that the Reformed people were no heretics.

to defect from the Roman Catholic church were ruthlessly and severely punished. And yet, in spite of the severity, the persecution was ineffective. Again and again new heretics were discovered. The priests, the executioners, and even the burning fagots could not terrorize them into giving up their new beliefs. Was the voice that spoke to them from the Bible, which also spoke in their hearts, the voice of God? Was this why they were able to endure suffering and even death? William did not understand. He had not heard that voice . . . yet. But the persecution threw a dark shadow on his merry life just as the thick smoke rising from the burning stakes darkened the sun.

*William of Orange* 1533 - 1584

## 6. Let Me Lean on Your Shoulder

The old man sat slumped in his beautiful chair. His gray head was bowed, his hands trembled, and his breathing was quick and uneven. His eyes gazed tiredly around the room.

The chair was splendid indeed, for it was the imperial throne. On the table next to it lay a golden crown sparkling with precious jewels. A velvet cap adorned the old, gray head, for the crown was too heavy for his head to bear. However, the crown was still his, symbol of his imperial power. The beautiful hall around which he gazed so sombrely was decked with a profusion of brilliant colours, of gold and rich velvets. Gathered in the hall were the most important men of the realm: bishops, rulers, and princes. All were clothed in rich and splendid garments. All stood in respect of the old one who sat on the throne.

Who was this old and pitiful man at the centre of attention surrounded by the choicest things the world could offer? He was none other than Charles V, the mightiest ruler in the world. With great difficulty, he rose from his seat. Standing was not easy, but his hand gripped the shoulder of the young man who stood at his side. On the emperor's other side stood his son Philip. Everyone watched the old ruler. Everyone waited respectfully to see what would happen. Bishops, knights, princes — all served the emperor. But who was the young man upon whose strong shoulder the emperor leaned so heavily? He was none other than William of Orange.

William was now a young man of twenty-two. He had been away, commanding soldiers of the imperial army in the war against the king of France. But the emperor had included the Prince of Orange when the leaders of his empire had been summoned. Leaving the clamour and excitement of a soldier's life behind, William hastened to Brussels. The emperor's wish was his command, and, perhaps, although it was a sad thought, it would be the last service he could perform for his beloved master.

So William stood, with the weight of the emperor leaning heavily on his shoulder. He stood in his rightful place as the man beloved and favoured by the emperor. William's heart ached with love and pity for his master. Actually, the emperor was not very old, having just celebrated his fifty-fifth birthday, but he looked like a crippled, gray-haired man of seventy.[1] His body was weak and sickly. He was tired of life. All the pomp and splendour and the homage of his people only served to tire him more. Ruling was too burdensome. He could no longer bear it. The heretics, deserters of the Roman Catholic church, were becoming too numerous. He had not succeeded in stemming the tide of the Reformation. Gallows, burning stakes, torture, rack, imprisonment — nothing had worked. It became a great source of bitterness and sorrow for him. He longed to be away from the turbulence and difficulties of life. He desired quiet, peace, and rest. In far-off Spain, he hoped to live a holy life in a secluded monastery where he could forget everything. Surrounded by pious monks he could draw closer to heaven, nearer to God, he thought.

Today he had assembled his men to inform them of his decision to abdicate. A strong, young man was needed to take his place. Philip, his son, would become king.[2] The old emperor spoke of his life, of the wars he had fought, and of the great power he held. But he also spoke of his physical weaknesses and old age. He assured them that Philip would be a

---

[1] Charles V was born in Ghent in 1500. In 1555 he abdicated as emperor in Brussels. He died in a Spanish palace in 1558 and was buried in the monastery of St. Juste.

[2] Philip did not become emperor of Germany as his father had been but received only the titles king of Spain and lord of the Netherlands. He also was ruler of Northern Italy and America. The leading German princes would choose another emperor themselves.

good king and asked them to honour and obey their new master as they had honoured and obeyed him. Finally, exhausted, he dropped back into his chair. Philip knelt, and the old emperor placed his hand upon his son's head in blessing.

The empire had received a new sovereign, but if he wished to speak to his subjects, he could not, for he spoke only Spanish, and the Dutch language was unfamiliar to him. It would be up to the Bishop of Granvelle to communicate with the people for him. This was not a good beginning for a new king.

William of Orange stood watching and listening carefully. His heart was full of compassion for the emperor as he asked them all to pledge their allegiance to their new king. The Prince of Orange was willing. He had always been the emperor's faithful servant and fully intended to serve Philip just as faithfully.

Then leaning heavily on William's arm, his other hand gripping a cane, the once powerful emperor limped out of the hall. What was left of all his glory? Nothing but a restless and embittered heart!

The following day William left Brussels to return to his troops. He belonged there. It was his rightful position as a faithful servant of his new king. He thought about his new master. Would he really be a good king? He had always been so quiet, so haughty. Would he place as much trust in William as his father had? He had always seemed so reserved and so suspicious of others. Would he deal better or worse with the heretics than his father had? Philip was a zealot and firmly believed the Roman church to be as heaven itself. What would happen now?

Of course William did not know the answers to his questions, but a tiny voice in his heart whispered a warning that the future could be dangerous. It was impossible to think happy, pleasant thoughts. Deep in sober meditation, William rode on.

## 7. The Parting of Ways

Four years later, in 1559, William was twenty-six. He wanted to be a faithful servant of his king, but what did that actually involve? Did that mean he was to do everything his lord and master asked? He shook his head. No, that could not be true. It was impossible to do everything. Even if the king commanded, it was not right to do anything wrong, wicked, or dishonest. Certainly William had vowed to serve as a faithful prince, but not with blind obedience. If a man ill-treated a little boy and set his dog upon him, the dog would attack, senselessly tearing at the boy's throat. This was blind obedience. People are not allowed to do this. They have to think, to use their minds. People are to have consideration for those who are weak and innocent. They have to question whether the orders given by their masters are in accordance with God's will. Should William be obedient to his master in everything? No, he did not think so. He was not allowed to.

William knew a dreadful secret. Each time he saw King Philip he would think about the secret and his heart grew angry. Feelings of compassion and distress awakened within him. Secretly he vowed, "I will never assist my king in such a vile, unjust matter!"

A splendid procession of blaring trumpets, waving banners, an abundance of rich velvets and silks, precious jewels, and beautiful apparel paraded through the streets. Sunlight glittered on burnished weapons and gleaming harnesses. In the distance, the sea shimmered softly. King Philip was going away. In Vlissingen he would board a ship for his beloved Spain. A great fleet of ships lay at anchor. They were laden with treasures. A splendid contingent of nobles came to the harbour to bid farewell to their king. William of Orange was there too. Why did he look so solemn?

Two columns of halberdiers with their weapons planted firmly at their feet stood as rigid as bronze statues while their ruler strode through their ranks. Beyond the soldiers and stretching far out along the beach, a crowd gathered, eager to see the spectacle. Were they also eager to pay their respectful farewells to their king? No indeed! He was returning to Spain. "Let him go!" No one mourned his departure. Although he had been king for four years and had lived among them for many more years, he had remained a stranger, a true Spaniard. He did not even understand the language. He did not care for these people, and the people did not care for him. "Let him go!"

If only he would take his Spanish soldiers along. But that was not to be the case. They were to stay behind. The people understood only too well. The soldiers were to keep the people fearful and apprehensive. Slowly they were to be deprived of their rights and freedoms. The soldiers had been given the power to seek out and exterminate the heretics.

Philip could not tolerate the Netherlanders speaking of their rights and privileges granted by former rulers and even by Charles V. Whenever Philip wanted to do something they did not like, they came with their old documents and protested. In Spain his will was law, his every command was carried out. But here . . . Yes, the Spanish soldiers must stay. Eventually this proud people would be humbled.

Philip could not stand it that so many people had turned their backs on the Roman Catholic church, insisting that they be allowed to serve God according to the voice of their own conscience. Fire and sword would get rid of those accursed heretics. Yes, the Spanish soldiers must stay. He, Philip, was the king; his will must be obeyed. The soldiers would see to it.

Philip longed for Spain. He had never felt at home here. Slowly he walked between the ranks of soldiers. A sneer played about his lips. He thought, I am leaving, yet I will remain in control. My power will grow stronger. I am lord, and these freedom-loving Netherlanders shall be my servants. My loyal soldiers will teach these arrogant people!

The war with France had ended. The seas were safe now so Philip dared to set sail for Spain. He was not a courageous man. However, the soldiers would remain to protect the borders, he explained, for France was not to be trusted.

At a meeting of the States'[1] representatives, he was outraged when they dared to ask that his soldiers be removed to Spain. His will was important, not theirs! What concern was it of his if the soldiers roamed the countryside ruthlessly plundering the towns and molesting the population? This nation of fishermen and cheesemongers deserved no better.

The king proceeded, a smirk on his lips. Beside him walked the Prince of Orange, his eyes sober. They were two men. The manner in which they walked together made it seem as though they were friends. Actually the king secretly hated the fine prince who walked at his side. He was jealous of William, who was so handsome and wise, so beloved by the people. On the other hand, William did not trust the cunning, ambitious monarch. He had a deep aversion for his king — and for that horrible secret! Two men — one great in power with a heart stripped bare of love and compassion, the other great in thoughtfulness, justice, and compassion. What did the future hold for these two men?

Behind them walked Margaret of Parma, the king's sister. She would rule as governess in Philip's stead. Orange was to be one of her advisors, assisting in her difficult task. Following Margaret in the procession were the Cardinal Granvelle, Count Egmond, and Count Horne together with a retinue of nobles and knights.

Suddenly Philip turned on William in fury and spat,

---

[1] This refers to the States-General, the parliament of the Netherlands.

"Not the States, but you, you, you!" Usually Philip was shrewd and kept his thoughts to himself, but at this moment he was overcome with bitterness and rage. How dare Orange ask yet once more on behalf of the States, for the sake of the people, that he withdraw his troops from the Netherlands?

The two men stood and stared at each other. The king's accusation was not true. The prince had not asked on his own behalf but out of concern for his people. His heart was heavy. That dreadful secret!

Yes, those two men understood each other well. The king, hated his people, while the other, only a stadtholder,[1] loved them. They could never be friends.

Prince William did not reply to the king's outburst; he maintained his silence. He did not know the king's plans, but he did not trust him.

Trumpets sounded and cannon boomed a final, farewell salute while colourful pennants fluttered in the breeze. The ships weighed anchor and set sail. Philip had quitted his country. He would never return, and the man who stood upon the seawall deep in thought would never see him again. As the fleet sailed out of the harbour, the distance between king and stadtholder grew ever wider. During the course of time, their aversion for one another would also grow, forcing them further apart. Today they had publicly appeared as friends. The day would come when they would be enemies. And then . . .?

Prince William stared pensively at the disappearing ships. He was thinking of the secret. There was a tale, which told of a meeting between Orange and the king of France. Not long ago, after the end of the war with France, William travelled to Paris. While out hunting with the French king he was asked, "So what do you think of this plan that Philip and

---

[1] governor

I have made?" The prince was unaware of any plan but he let the king continue speaking. Thus he heard what he should never have known.

The two kings, Philip of Spain and Henry II of France, promised never to go to war against each other again. Rather they conspired to wage another kind of war. Now they were in league to fight a cruel and merciless battle against the heretics. Neither would rest or give up until that battle had been won, until the last man, woman, and child who professed the new faith had been ruthlessly put to death by fire, drowning, or gallows. This was the dreadful secret William bore.[1]

Yes, Philip had left, but the soldiers remained, and so Philip's merciless power remained also. What a stricken people to have such a king!

But William had also remained. Of course he was not a king. He was only a knight of the royal court, an advisor to the governess, an ordinary stadtholder who must carry out his master's orders. What could he do? His noble heart would love those poor, unfortunate people and his intelligent mind would carefully consider various ways of softening the king's cruelty. In his brutal ambition for power, the king had turned away from his people in peevish spite. The prince, a wise statesman, turned to his people in compassion. Thus the two men were separated. King Philip had left many orders for his men. William, too, had received final instructions. He shuddered. Certain respected men and women living in his territory were under suspicion for being heretics and were to be taken captive. This was the king's will, and Orange, as stadtholder, must obey. William would begin with this task. He had to. But . . .

Soldiers marched to the homes of the heretics to arrest them. However, when they arrived, they found that the people had fled. How was that possible? Out of compassion, the prince had forewarned them of the danger that threatened. Because he considered it was right to do the will of God before the will of man, he had helped save their lives. The brutal murder of innocent people could certainly never be God's will.

---

[1] This secret caused William of Orange to be remembered as William the Silent.

## 8. In the Quiet Council Chamber

A rich and happy life — what else could a man want? William of Orange was twenty-six and possibly the wealthiest man in Brussels. He was certainly the most well known, for who in Brussels did not know the Prince of Orange? Who had never heard of the sumptuous, splendid feasts given in his palace, the castle of the Nassau's? And who did not know that he was a caring, generous, and friendly man? In Brussels he lived royally. Everyone liked him. Certainly this was much better than being a wealthy landowner of far off Dillenburg in the heart of quiet farming territory. This wonderful life would continue and become ever more grand. William was a wise man, a good counsellor. Fortune seemed to smile on him. The highest position in the land, great wealth, high esteem, and great power could all be his if . . . if William of Orange carried out the will of the new king. Already he was stadtholder of Holland, Zealand, and Utrecht as well as advisor to the governess. He could become more important, even the most important man in the country if . . . if he assisted the king in depriving the Netherlanders of their old rights and freedoms and rid the land of heretics and heresy.

If . . . But William refused. What a foolish man! He was so clever and cautious. He could do much better than Philip himself. Then he would definitely receive the highest honour, the greatest power of his life. But he refused. Foolish man! What did the people matter to him? They could not give him greatness and glory. Only the king could do that. Forget the people. What did it matter to him if they lost their freedom and became a nation of slaves as the Spanish people were under the command of Philip? Why should he be concerned about the heretics? They were only strangers to him. He did not know the men and women who paid the price of their faith with their lives. He, wealthy prince, lived in his royal residence or stayed in the grand palace of Margaret, the governess. He celebrated the tournaments with splendour and pomp and rode on exciting hunts. Could he feel the pain inflicted on the poor victims condemned to the scaffold or the stake? Could he hear the moans and anguished cries of those in agony? Did he understand the deep grief suffered by those who saw father, mother, child, or wife taken away by the executioner? What did this sorry lot of humanity have to do with him? He, was safe. He was not one of the heretics. He was a happy man who enjoyed his wonderful life.

Then why did he not obey the king? Why did he constantly consider the needs of his people? Why was he worried about the terrorized lives of the heretics? These concerns only hindered his progress in gaining greatness and power. They overshadowed his happy life. Foolish man!

Now he stood in Margaret's council chamber. The governess sat at the head of the table surrounded by her advisors. There was Barlaimont, the king's faithful follower, who shared the king's hatred for the heretics. There was Viglius, a Frisian who cared more for his own ambitions and honour than for his people. Then there was Horne, an awkward man, the Prince's friend.

Orange stood, looking earnestly at the governess. Anger blazed in his dark eyes. In grave tones he said, "This cannot continue! I am Roman Catholic, but I do not find it acceptable for the king to rule the consciences of his people and deprive them of the freedom to believe and worship God in the way they believe to be right!"

There he stood with arms outstretched as if embracing his people, shielding them from the cunning cruelty of Viglius and the others, protecting them from the king's hatred. William had spoken openly. Philip was a wicked king serving his people badly. He, William of Orange, wanted to help them.

Margaret felt her mouth tremble in shock. "How dare the Prince of Orange speak thus?"

Viglius, himself a son of these oppressed people, was required, as secretary, to deliver this harsh message to the king. His heart shrank in fear.[1] How dare Orange speak out against the king? How dare he oppose the mighty King Philip? It was extremely dangerous. He would place his whole life in jeopardy!

Why had William dared to speak out? His heart was stirred with compassion for the stricken, oppressed people. He was filled with anger against the king's unfairness. William could not allow himself to be the Spanish king's puppet. His noble heart could not endure the falseness, cruelty, and injustice. He had heard the cries that rose up from the land. He had seen the pain, the sorrow, the misery everywhere. Now, here in this quiet council chamber, he had taken his stand. In the towns and villages, people were unaware that William was fighting to protect and defend their rights. Their champion was only a young prince. Could he really help? This young prince

---

[1] Viglius did not recover from the shock of William's words. The following day he suffered a stroke and died.

was still unaware that he would be a hero. After all, he was only an advisor, and the king was so powerful. However, God in heaven knew, for He alone determines the destinies of people — even of kings and emperors and nations according to His holy will. Was it not this same God who worked the love and courage in the young prince's heart? Orange stood in the quiet council chamber in the service of God, although he did not realize it. Who did realize this? Sometimes things happen in mysterious and wondrous ways. Orange had come from Germany as a little boy-prince. He bore a French name, Orange. And now he had demonstrated a Dutch heart. How strange! Yet the God in heaven knew why. In the quiet council chamber William had spoken the courageous words, "This cannot continue!" Selflessly he had placed the needs of the people before his own, with no regard for his own honour or happiness. It seemed foolish, but he could not, nor would he do otherwise. Orange would persevere. God would give him the strength and will, although he did not yet realize it.

## 9. That Noble, Generous Heart . . .
## Who Could Understand It?

Orange smiled to himself. It had been a very good day. Years of stealthy, bitter conflict had passed. He was now thirty-three years old. Everyone knew that he was not a friend of the king. They also knew that he did all he could to help his people. And today?

Today an endless procession of noblemen had ridden through the streets of Brussels to the palace of the governess. Many had been attired in shabby and worn-out garments. Crowds had gathered and lined the streets to watch the procession with new hope in their hearts. Everyone had known the procession's destination and purpose. It was to appeal to the governess, to present her with the Petition of the Noblemen. She would be told of the great need of the people, of their suffering and misery. She would also be made aware of the quiet but growing rage that was sweeping the country. Counts, earls, dukes, and barons, all leaders of the land, Roman Catholics and those who embraced the new faith, gathered to ask Margaret to show compassion and halt the persecution of the heretics. They came to present all people. Margaret and the king would have to listen.

Louis of Nassau, Prince William's younger brother, and Henry of Brederode had led the delegation together with the highest leaders of the land. What about the Prince of Orange? He had not accompanied them, although he did belong with them. He was, in fact, their leader. However, he was also one of Margaret's advisors. He could not approach her as a petitioner.

Yes, William smiled. It had indeed been a good day. The governess had been deeply alarmed. She had accepted the document from Brederode's hand. Her face had gone pale and

her lips had trembled.

Barlaimont, one of her most faithful aides, had only smiled derisively at the poorly clad messengers. He had leaned forward and whispered loudly, "My lady, why are you so upset? After all, they are only beggars."

Margaret had promised to read the petition and give an answer later. The delegation had left the palace in triumph. Brussels had been filled with celebrating. New hope had been born in the hearts of the people. If only the king would listen, they would obey him as faithful, grateful subjects.

A few days later another celebration took place. The nobility came from all directions to gather at a prominent home in Brussels. Savel Street was not particularly fashionable, but some very influential people lived there. Floris of Pallant, Count of Kuilenburg, the wealthiest knight of the Netherlands, owned the house on the corner now patrolled by sentries. In this distinguished building an alliance of the nobility had been formed, and from here the splendid procession had gone forth to the palace of the governess. It was this event that would now be celebrated. Brederode was to preside over the gathering, and together they would commemorate true unity and friendship.

The feasting grew merry. Brederode stood up. About his neck he had hung a gray linen sack, a real beggar's sack. It was a double sack with one compartment hanging forward on his chest and the other draped over his back. Tramps wore similar sacks while roaming the streets and countryside. Next Brederode held up a wooden dish filled with wine, a real beggar's bowl. His eyes gleamed in mockery, but his face was serious.

"We have been called beggars," he said, "but the name 'beggars' will become our name of honour.[1]" He continued,

---

[1] Barlaimont had spoken to Margaret in French. In this language the term *beggars* is *les gueux*.

"We will be faithful to the king, but we will do everything possible to win freedom of conscience, even if it means becoming as poor as beggars. The beggar's sack and the beggar's bowl will become our symbols of honour!" Brederode then drained the cup. "Long live the beggars!" he shouted.

"Long live the beggars!" resounded throughout the hall.

The beggar's bowl was filled with wine and passed around. Everyone drank from it.

"'Beggar' shall be our name of honour. We shall all carry a medal. The king's likeness shall be engraved on one side, and on the reverse, a beggar's sack with two hands joined together in trust. The text to be inscribed shall be 'Faithful to

the king unto beggary'."

"Vivent les gueux — long live the beggars!"

The celebrating grew noisier and rowdier. All the men were friends. They felt brave and strong. They would do great things!

Later that afternoon, Prince William arrived at the feast with some of his close friends. Standing, he drank a glass of wine. He too belonged. He was welcomed with loud joyous cries. Everyone considered him to be the strongest man, not in physical strength, but in wisdom. A head of wisdom was of more benefit than brawn. But William, always so thoughtful and careful with words, who considered and reconsidered before he spoke, secretly shook his head. Oh yes, fine, brave words had been spoken here today, and there was an abundance of zeal. But would the men remain faithful to these words when put to the test? Loud shouting and cheering at a feast was easy, but to do the deeds, to perform one's utmost for this great cause, would be difficult. Yet the prince was happy. This alliance of the noblemen could be a good beginning.[1]

---

[1] The alliance of the noblemen did not accomplish much. Margaret promised moderation in the persecution, but the people called it *murderation*.

Some time later, Orange smiled to himself and said to his best friend, Marnix of St. Aldegonde, "Yes, matters are proceeding well."

William was thinking of the hundreds, the thousands, of people who came from the great cities of Antwerp, Leiden, Alkmaar, and Utrecht to gather in the fields. Some carried weapons. Was it their intention to stir up trouble or to fight? No. They gathered in the woods around some farmer's covered wagon. In the wagon, shaded from the sun, stood a simple man, a preacher. Everyone listened intently to him. They sang and prayed. This was a "hedge service," an assembly of the heretics in the open air, for they had no churches in the big cities. At first they had gathered in small groups in cellars or attics and in abandoned sheds to read the Bible and pray together, to worship God in earnest, sincere devotion. They were however in great danger of being betrayed. If discovered, they would be tortured and put to death as disobedient traitors. But the heretics had become brave. They flocked to the hedge services held in the country. Many of the men carried weapons to guard the crowds. If the governess's soldiers should appear, the guards would fight. For now, they listened and prayed.

The Prince of Orange had heard of these hedge services. He smiled. First an alliance of the nobility, now the hedge services. Of course matters were proceeding well!

But were they really? The alliance was important. The

47

nobles were gallant and rich, trained soldiers. They could be worth something to this crushed land. But the pious, devout people who listened to the preacher's words — what could they do with their songs and their prayers against the evil, cunning Philip and his soldiers, who knew no mercy?

William of Orange was a wise man. He realized that the strong, deep faith of the devout people participating in the hedge services could be more of a threat to Philip than all the uproar caused by the bold knights. The people fully trusted in God. They would persevere and sacrifice everything necessary to obtain freedom of conscience. They would suffer and die for their faith. They knew their weaknesses, but they also knew that God was powerful.

The governess would not suddenly crush the hedge services. She did not dare. Orange was glad. The governess would realize that the whole nation, knights and commoners, Roman Catholics and heretics — all belonged together and would not simply bow to King Philip's wicked will.

The people who followed the new religion had already requested church buildings in which to worship. Their requests had not been approved, but they would be. They had to be. Roman Catholics and Reformed could live side-by-side in the same towns and cities as friends.

These were the thoughts of the noble, generous heart of Orange. He did not realize that he was alone in the world. The people of his time could not understand his noble, generous heart. The Roman Catholics knew that Orange was also a Roman Catholic, yet he did everything he could to help the heretics. How was that possible? The heretics knew Orange was their friend, yet he remained a Roman Catholic. How was that possible? Many people decided he was indifferent and could not make up his mind.

Quietly, William of Orange continued in his own way with courage. His great task was done in silence.

## 10. The Storm Which Spoiled Everything

What a horrible shock! Orange's eyes were sombre, afraid, and angry. Finally he gave the order, "Pursue the troublemakers! Find them! They shall not escape punishment!"

The prince's messengers hastened to carry his orders to all the cities and towns of which Orange was stadtholder. It was too late. The violence was history. A fierce storm is over quickly. It comes up suddenly, rages violently, and destroys everything. It leaves only a trail of wretchedness and destruction.

And so it had been with the "image-breaking wave"[1] in 1566. It had arisen on the flat lands of West Flanders. In Antwerp it had raged most fiercely. How had it really begun? No one knew. Some mischief-makers had entered the beautiful cathedral of *Our Beloved Lady* causing a disturbance during the worship service. They had been thrown out but had returned the following day. Who had thrown the first stone through the beautiful stained glass windows? Who had torn the costly cloth from the altar and soiled it with muddy boots? And who had been the first to smash one of the beautiful holy images to pieces? It had become a scene of frenzied madness.

One church after another had been ravaged by the angry mob. They ruthlessly spoiled and shattered everything beautiful and precious. Everything symbolic of the Roman Catholic church had to be destroyed. Nothing had been taken as loot. Everything had been demolished.

One town followed another. In a matter of a few days the contents of hundreds of churches were ruined.

Who had done this? The heretics, it was said.

---

[1] Iconoclastic movement.

But certainly not those quiet, devout people drawn to God in love. Rather it was the hotheaded fanatics who had risen in bitter hatred against the Roman hierarchy. They were the roughnecks and rogues and the noisy, clamorous throngs of the markets who thought that destruction was a show of bravery. They screamed, "We want churches just as well as the Romanists. Away with the idols, away with the saints-shop!"

After the churches had been laid waste, the religious houses, monasteries, and convents were attacked. The image-breaking wave rampaged like a contagious disease. But a violent storm does not last long. It had arisen swiftly, raged violently and destroyed everything. In its wake lay mounds of rubble. The holy images, the beautiful paintings, and the sacred, golden ornaments of the churches had been destroyed. But that was not all. Something else had also been destroyed, something much more precious.

William of Orange, rich, happy, powerful prince, sat at his table deep in thought. His great, wonderful plan had failed. A wide, deep chasm had split the Roman Catholic Church and the Reformed Churches. Everything had been rent in two. Philip would have an easier time making these people his slaves. Orange's heart was filled with anger against the fools who had destroyed so much and gained nothing. Now those good, peaceable, devout people, the innocent, would have to suffer with those who were guilty. Orange knew one thing for sure. The king's vengeance would be terrible. When he thought about it, that old, familiar, warm, compassionate feeling for the people of the Netherlands was foremost in his heart. A good, loving father could also have reason to be angry with his son who had misbehaved. He would punish him, perhaps even severely. But at the same time he would feel sadness and compassion. A father would not hate his son but love him as before. He would be anxiously asking, "What will become of my wild and headstrong son? The world is so cruel and men have no mercy. I will certainly do what I can for my foolish son." This was how a father would think. And this was also the manner of Prince William's thoughts.

But now what about Philip, the King, the real father of these people? When he had heard of the image-breaking wave he had been greatly alarmed. A wild rage had possessed him.

Gnashing his teeth, he had flung his royal headdress on the floor and stomped on it. He had burst out, "By my mother's soul, I vow to repay those people. And not only those accursed heretics, but also the others, the Roman Catholics as well! How could they have allowed such sacrilegious destruction of those beautiful churches." Philip wanted no part of forgiveness.

Sometime in the future one of these two men, Philip or Orange, would bear the name, "Father of the Fatherland." Who would it be?

## 11. Calm and Heroic

"Forward! Through the gate! Kill! Kill the papists!"

The frenzied throng forced its way through the narrow streets of Antwerp and climbed, shrieking and screaming, upon the city walls. Outside on the open green fields a battle had been fought. A small group of the governess' soldiers had overtaken a group of beggars and cut them down. The result was a horrible blood bath.

"Must we simply stand by and watch?" came a cry from the city wall. "Storm the gate! Kill! Death to the papists!"

From the streets and alleys poured the hundreds and thousands of people who had renounced the Roman religion and meant to win their freedom through rebellion and disobedience. Pikes, spears, axes, pitchforks, sledgehammers, and knives were raised high amid the clamour of cries, "Kill! Avenge our comrades!"

Suddenly, at the gate, in the midst of the fierce outcry, a strange hush swept through the crowd. Weapons were lowered. The frenzied shouting died down. A horseman approached — a knight who rode straight into the surging crowd. The people pushed and shoved to get a better look and demanded, "Who is it?"

The mounted knight was Prince William of Orange. He raised his hand asking for silence. His dark eyes gazed calmly at the restless men and women commanding silence. But then, suddenly, the crowd surged forward angrily against him. They shook their fists and brandished their weapons high in the air.

"Traitor", they screamed. "Rogue and traitor!"

A man called out, "It is his fault that our brothers are slain beyond the walls. He must die. Yes! He, too, shall die!" The crazed man then raised his gun and took aim. Just in time, another pushed the weapon aside. The prince's life was spared.

The prince's reaction was unexpected. Rather than feeling fear, anger, or shock, he felt only deep compassion for the rebellious people. He did not run in fear of his life but stayed and asked for silence.

Gradually the noise died down, and he began to speak. He insisted that he was not a traitor. If he could have saved those who had been cut down in the field, he would have done so. But it had been impossible. Now the rioting crowd, determined to avenge their brothers, could only meet with failure. The well trained troops of the governess would cut them down as well. The prince urged them to stop and offered to help them if they would be quiet and listen. His words appeared to have effect on his hearers. The people respected his fearlessness. There were many honest and sincere men and women in the crowd who liked the prince. But there were also many rebels who were driven by hatred against the Roman church and its priests; they were convinced that riches were acquired through rebellion and looting. However, the majority did listen. Only a small group of fools persisted in escaping through the gate, but they were quickly persuaded by the soldiers to beat a hasty retreat.

The prince rode on to the town hall to consult with the town leaders. He hated the senseless rioting, for it would only cause more trouble for the people. For the remainder of the day and throughout the night, the grumbling and discontented rebels remained in the market square. Often they shouted, "Death to the papists! Life to the beggars!"

Fear gripped the city. The rebellious mob threatened to plunder the homes of the Roman Catholics and murder or drive the owners away.

"Away with the papists!"

The uproar swelled; Orange grew adamant and remained watchful. The uprising must be put down. He assembled the Roman Catholics and other citizens who did not want to participate in the rebellion. He watched and waited all day and all night. At dawn he returned to the angry mob. His life was in jeopardy, yet William stood unafraid, and warned the people to go home.

"A horrible blood bath will come upon this city bringing grief and misery if you do not go home. I will do what I can for you."

The heated crowd was unwilling and resentful. At last they responded; they trusted Prince William. At first only a few left, but gradually more followed and went home. The uprising was over.

The prince had restored peace in Antwerp. He had spared the people from certain death, grief, and misery. They were all men and women of the same nation. Was it necessary to fight and destroy each other? Today he had helped Romanists and Protestants alike. But were the people grateful? No, for they could not understand the great, noble heart of Orange.

The Protestants said, "He is a friend of the Roman Catholics. He has protected them."

The Roman Catholics claimed, "He is a friend of the Protestants. He has promised to help them."

And the governess thought, He cares for the heretics. I do not trust him.

The noble Prince of Orange was misunderstood by everyone. And yet he would risk his own life for his people. A sad smile hovered on his lips as he thought, I will not let what others say bother me, and I will never fear their hatred. With a clear conscience and a courageous heart, I must continue to do what is right.

## 12. Exiled!

A horseman travelled through the countryside of Germany. He rode with head bowed low, thoughtful and dispirited. He was a man of importance, yet he was a fugitive. A small troop accompanied him. Wagons loaded with valuable possessions followed.

The man raised his head. In the distance he could see the towers and battlements of a castle outlined against the sky. He smiled sadly and thought, Do I have to return to my old home in this way? Have I failed? Must those good people, that poor nation, bow under the yoke of the cruel king after all?

He was deeply grieved, but as he neared the castle happy thoughts blocked the sorrow from his mind. The castle was the strong, secure Dillenburg where his old mother now awaited his arrival. And he — a great, strong man, proud knight, and wealthy prince — longed to see his old mother.

The fugitive was William of Orange. King Philip II had sent the Duke of Alva with a formidable army of Spanish soldiers to the Netherlands. The duke was not a compassionate man. For those people who were called beggars the punishment would be terribly severe. Rich and poor, old and young; all who had at times attended the hedge services, or had sung the Protestant hymns or Psalms, or had read the Bible, or had disobeyed the priests in any way would pay heavily. They were to be arrested and hanged, drowned, or burned. And if there was a shortage of wood for constructing gallows, well, there were plenty of trees lining the roads. Philip's revenge would be fierce and relentless. Alva would spare no one. He would establish a new court of justice. The Council Against Disturbances would bring to justice and punish all those responsible for the turmoil caused by the heretics. But the new court would soon become known as the Council of Blood.

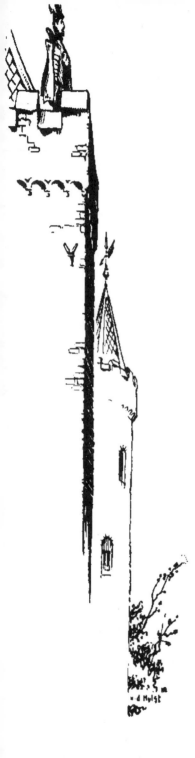

Thousands, including the Prince of Orange, had fled their country.

William knew his life was in grave danger. At Dillenburg he would be safe. Alva could not reach him there. But what had become of his greatness, wealth, and power? The prince was not concerned about them. Other matters were more important and weighed heavily on his mind.

That evening he stood once more upon the ramparts of the castle. He had stood there years before as a young boy. And now, as then, he turned his gaze westward. The sun had already disappeared beneath the horizon. The golden light of sunset was fading. Soon darkness would fall. On that evening so long ago, William had not known the lowlands by the sea. He had only been a young boy. Now he knew the lands and the people who lived there. He knew their suffering and anguish, the oppression by their own king. Their pain was also William's. Soberly his eyes watched the encroaching darkness. The last faint glow of light disappeared. Darkness fell over the land.

Yes, that was how it was. The darkness of misery and oppression had settled over the land with the arrival of the Duke of Alva. Would light ever return? Orange clenched his fists, anger flared in his eyes. He was a German prince who bore a French name, but his heart belonged to Holland. He cared deeply for those people of the lowlands. Would this nation now have to disappear, ransacked and murdered? Was there no one willing to help them? Then William of Orange raised his head. His expression was grim and resolute. He whispered aloud, *"Je maintiendrai!*[1] With God's help I will persevere. I will do whatever I can and give whatever I have. Now I am a fugitive in exile. But I will sacrifice everything I have: my youth, my goods, my strength, my wisdom, my blood, even my life if necessary. Alva, . . . I have not been defeated yet!"

During the dark, sad days at Dillenburg, at home with his devout mother, a great thankfulness filled William's heart. Now, more than in those bygone days of a wonderful life full of pleasure and luxuries, the prince felt close to God. Here in the words and prayers of his old mother he found comfort. She often consoled him. "Our heavenly Father guides our lives. He will not forget or abandon us — not even when we are in dire need."

Here the prince learned to seek strength and comfort from God. Here he learned to pray as he had never prayed before. Suffering and hardship brought him closer to God.

One cold January morning in the year 1568, six trumpeters accompanied a herald to the front entrance of the palace in Brussels. The people stood watching and listening. Trumpets sounded. Then the messenger proclaimed the edict of

---

[1] I will maintain, or, I will persevere. The motto of the House of Orange.

*Alvarez de Toledo, Duke of Alva* (1508 - )

Alva so all could hear. "Prince William has been commanded
to appear before the Council against Disturbances. Those who
heard were stunned. Would Orange obey? If so, then all was
over for the Prince.

The messenger read on saying that Orange was the most
dangerous rebel, the leader of the riots which had plagued the
country. He, together with his brother Louis and many other
leading knights, were enemies of the people and had destroyed
their orderly way of life. They had all been ordered to appear

before Alva's court. He would pronounce judgment and uphold justice.

Justice! Those who listened were tempted to scream, Justice! That is a lie! But they dared not. Traitors lurked everywhere. The people knew that Alva and his henchmen were cruel and dishonest. Those who were wealthy had not the slightest chance for escape. Even if their lives were spared, they would still be condemned and forced to pay a heavy penalty. All their possessions and money would be confiscated by Alva. He and his king hungered for gold.

Would Orange obey the summons? No, he would not appear before Alva's court. That would mean certain death. When Orange received Alva's message, he shook his head in anger. How dare the haughty duke write this? Was Alva the master and he the servant? Could Alva command for him to obey? No! Orange was a prince, higher in status than Alva. He was a knight of the Golden Fleece, an association of the highest ranking nobles. If one misbehaved, he would be examined and judged by his peers. Prince William did not have to appear before a foreign judge. So he had answered Alva's summons with a proud and spirited reply.

Then Alva pronounced judgment on William, but Orange had disappeared. Alva then proceeded to confiscate the lands and castles in the Netherlands that belonged to the prince. Worse yet, and this had been done by the king's decree, Prince William's young son, Philip William, a student at the University of Louvain near Brussels, was taken to Spain. Father and son never saw each other again.

Thus Philip took revenge on the prince who refused to come before Alva's court. Alva was very powerful but knew no compassion. He sneered, "I have conquered a people of iron with my fist. Shall I not master this land of butter?"[1] What had Philip to fear from a prince without land or wealth?

On a fine, clear day in April, just as William was returning to Dillenburg from a day of hunting, a group of people stood waiting for him under the great green leafy linden tree close to the castle. They bowed before William, with shining eyes of joy and hope. The prince recognized them and the language they spoke. His eyes lit up in gladness. They were Netherlanders. They had come as ambassadors on behalf of their oppressed and tormented country. They asked him to return. There were many ready and willing to fight against the tyranny of Philip and Alva, but there was no one to lead them and give direction. He, the Prince of Orange, could guide them. Next to God, they placed their hope and trust in him.

Orange listened, deeply moved. The old love in his heart blazed up anew. Would he go? Would he help? He would no longer be a fugitive but an acknowledged opponent of Alva. It was a dangerous plan. He would not be able to go alone. That would cost him his life. He would have to lead a mighty army. His eyes shone, and his heart ached with longing. He could, he would, he was not allowed to refuse. He would go to the Netherlands. Although the way was not yet clear he was willing to do his best. He had to.

"I will come."

---

[1] Alva meant: In the past I won the victory over the Turks, though they were a lot stronger than the farmers in the Netherlands.

## 13. "Thy Will Be Done"

"Forward!"

Leading an army, William of Orange marched from Germany into the Netherlands. The plumes on his helmet waved in the wind. His eyes sparkled with zeal and courage. Now, if the people of the Netherlands would help him, then together they could drive out the tyrant. If only the people could understand the great love the prince had for them and their country.

He rode at the head of an army. Where had it come from? Orange had hired the soldiers for great sums of money. At that time this was possible. There were enough men willing to fight for a knight who was willing to pay handsomely. They were mercenaries, and fighting was their trade. Cannon and muskets, swords and trumpets, horses, wagons, tents, and other implements of war could be bought for a lot of money. William of Orange had sold all his treasures and his household silver to get enough money. His former power and glory had been lost. He had become a fugitive. He could not accept King Philip's harsh treatment of these people. So William had sold everything he owned. He became poor so he could help his people.

Foolish man! Did he not have to consider his own benefit, his own importance, his own happiness? Why not forget about those people? Many others would have done so. But the noble heart of Orange could not. He would risk everything.

"Forward!"

But then, bitter disappointment! Lost, lost, everything was lost! The people of the Netherlands had not dared support him. The terror and fear of the Spanish tyrant was too deeply imbedded in their hearts. They did not dare rise up to help their prince.

Louis of Nassau, William's brother, had led a small army into the province of Groningen and had defeated the Spanish close to Heiligerlee. It had been a victorious beginning. But in that battle, Adolf of Nassau, William's brother, was slain. He was the first son of Juliana of Stolberg to sacrifice his life for the cause of the people of the Netherlands.

Then Alva had gone to Groningen himself. However, before leaving Brussels, he had beheaded Count Egmond and Count Horne. This move was to serve as an example for the people and to strike fear deeper into their hearts. Even the greatest, the nobility of the land, were not spared.

At Jemmingen, Louis' army had been miserably beaten. He ran out of money to pay the hired soldiers. They had fled. Count Louis, himself, had been forced to flee. In the dense brush he had hastily unbuckled his suit of armour, thrown it away, and crossed the Eems River to save his life.

Prince William had ridden into Brabant. When Alva heard of it he exclaimed, "That is impossible! Orange would have had to lead his army across the mighty Maas River, and soldiers are not geese which can fly!"

But it was true. It had been a brilliant piece of military strategy, the crossing of a reasonably shallow section of the Maas River. First, the mounted men had entered the water in a broad row to create a crude dam. Alongside this dam, the foot soldiers had forded the river. At times the water reached the soldiers necks, but the force of the current was broken by the horses — thus saving the men from being carried downstream.

The words *Pro Lege, Rege, et Grege*! — for the Law, the King, and the People — were written on the banners of the prince's army.

"But if they indeed crossed the River," said Alva, "then I will indeed break that arrogant Orange's spirit!"

But did the duke then march with his soldiers into battle with the prince's army to defeat him? Oh no, the clever tyrant had devised a much better way. He had known very well that William's hired mercenaries would fight only as long as they were paid. He had also known that the prince lacked funds. Alva had been willing to meet the prince in battle, but he preferred not to do any real fighting. So instead, he drew nearer to the prince's army and then evaded real combat with the soldiers who fought only for pay. Finally the prince's money had been exhausted, and his soldiers refused to obey his commands.

Those had been bitter days for the Prince of Orange. The crude, greedy soldiers, had intended to fight only for personal gain, to seize booty through raiding and plundering. They were after excitement and adventure. The plight of the Netherlanders meant nothing to them. They were a mixture of German, French, and Italian soldiers. Why should they concern themselves with Orange's problems? What did they care of his noble ideals or the love in his heart? Money! Loot! Excitement! These were what they lived for. And if he could not pay them

. . .

In the midst of this crude lot, William's life had often been in great danger. His money was gone and their rebelliousness grew worse and worse, until, at last, they had deserted him.

This had been Alva's great victory.

Orange had been forced to flee to France. Everything had begun so well at Heiligerlee. But the brave had been slain, the knights, had been murdered, the prince had fled, and the people had been enslaved. Alva jeered. He had achieved his goal. In a letter to a friend, he had written, "The Prince of Orange is a dead man." That appeared to be true.

The burning stakes continued to smoulder, blood poured from the scaffolds, and corpses hung from trees lining the roads. Lost — everything had been lost!

William wrote in a letter to his mother. "I realize that I must spend my life in poverty and misery, but, if it pleases the Almighty, I will accept that. If only He will give me the patience to bear it."

His mother read the letter and remembered the day so long ago when she had stood praying beside his cradle. How had that innocent, young, life which had begun so wonderfully become so difficult. And yet, in her sorrow and anxiety, there came a calm, happy thought. Her son had lost much, but he had won far more. He had gained something much greater than all the richest treasures or the highest honours. He was a child of God. He was no longer indifferent; he firmly rejected the heresies of the Roman Catholic church. He had become one of the oppressed people. At last he had learned to place his trust in God. And she, old, sorrowful woman that she was, what could she do for him now? Her son Adolf, whom she also loved very much, was dead. He was the first to go. Would more of her sons have to give their lives for this cause? Her motherly heart cringed.

"Lord, Thy will be done. Grant me peace. Let me never, never doubt Thy goodness and wisdom. Hear my prayers, for my sons as well as for those poor people."

Was everything lost? In those days it certainly seemed

so. It was as though God had spoken, "Not in this way. Trust in me."

William of Orange and his brothers had done what they could.

*But to the Lord, the greatest*
*Of majesties, I owe*
*Obedience first and latest,*
*For justice wills it so.*

## 14. The Most Beautiful Song of the Netherlands[1]

Prince William had many friends. His friends were among the prominent and distinguished families as well as among the humble folk who lived in the country cottages. One of his most faithful friends was Marnix of St. Aldegonde: a gallant knight, a noble gentleman, a true Christian. He was a member of the prince's defeated army. He, also, had been forced to flee for his life. Yet he wanted to help the prince.

Marnix sat alone in his quiet chamber. He wrote poetry and was composing something for his friend. How could this help William of Orange? Marnix understood his friend. He liked and admired William and now his heart reached out to him. The misery and frustration, the love and faithfulness, his trust in God — everything that was part of the prince was shared by Marnix of St. Aldegonde. And so he composed his verses. It was wonderful work, for he wrote as though Prince William spoke the words himself.

When he had finished he took the paper to the prince. It was only paper with some short lines written on it, but he believed it would help his friend.

"I have something to read to you," said Marnix.

"William of Nassau, scion
Sprung of an ancient line . . ."

The prince looked up in wonder. This was a poem about himself, but written as though he was speaking!

---

[1] This song — a Reformed confession — has become the national anthem of the Netherlands. In this chapter we are following the translation by A.J. Barnouw. At the end of this book the complete text is printed in both English and Dutch.

"I dedicate undying
Faith to this land of mine. . ."

William nodded in agreement.

"A prince I am, undaunted,
Of Orange, ever free.[1]
The king of Spain I've granted
My lifelong loyalty. . ."

Yes, certainly he wanted to be his king's loyal servant,
but . . .

"I've ever tried to live in
The fear of God's command,
And therefore I've been driven
From people, home, and land. . ."

The prince became sad. He thought, I still love my
people. The beautiful poem continued.

"He who would live devoutly
Must pray God day and night
To throw his power about me
As champion of your right. . ."

The verse also spoke of sad things . . .

"Count Adolf, more's the pity,
Fell in the Frisian fray . . .[2]

---

[1] Free: William was sovereign Prince of Orange

[2] The province of Groningen where Count Adolf died used to be part of Friesland.

William remembered that dreadful battle and thought, too, of his grieving mother. Yet, his great love for his suffering people overcame even his personal sorrow.

> "O that the Spaniards rape thee,
> My Netherlands so sweet —
> The thought of that does grip me,
> Causing my heart to bleed. . ."

Then he recalled his flight from Alva.

> "Once David searched for shelter
> From King Saul's tyranny.
> E'en so I fled this welter
> And many a lord with me. . ."

William's thoughts dwelt on that army that had so valiantly entered the country but that had been so wretchedly beaten. Oh yes, Orange longed to help that suffering and oppressed nation.

> "But He who dwells in heaven,
> Whence all our blessings flow,
> For which aye praise be given,
> Did not desire it so. . ."

The prince bowed his head. No, it had not been the Lord's will. But even the misery and oppression were a part of His plan, His will. He, William of Orange, must be patient, thankful, and faithful, placing his trust in the God of heaven and earth.

"A shield and my reliance,
O God, Thou ever wert.
I'll trust unto Thy guidance.
O leave me not ungirt,
That I may stay a pious
Servant of Thine for aye,
And drive the plagues that try us
And tyranny away."

And so the beautiful poem became a prayer. Silently William sat with his head bowed. He was very sad. Yet William was firmly convinced with the wonderful belief that the Lord would not forsake those persecuted people! Secretly he vowed never to lose courage, regardless of how difficult his life became. He would sacrifice everything to win freedom for his people. God would stand by him. Listening to the poem, it was as though he had received comfort and encouragement from heaven. He stood up. The old, familiar, fiery spirit glowed in his eyes. Unshakable confidence burned in his heart.

"*Je maintiendrai*! I will persevere!"

Thus the simple verses became a source of comfort for Orange. In this way, Marnix of St. Aldegonde helped him far more than he ever could in battle.

The poem became known throughout the land. Before long it was being sung to the tune of a familiar French song. This was how "Wilhelmus" became the national anthem of the Netherlands. It had been born from sorrow and suffering. For centuries it has remained a hymn and prayer, in times of rejoicing and in times of adversity. Still, today, it lives on. This beautiful anthem is as much a part of the people of the Netherlands as William of Orange. The most beautiful song of the Netherlands shall never be taken from her.

## 15. A Critical Struggle

There were very difficult years in the prince's life. But sometimes some light would shine through the darkness. It was 1572.

"I do want to help, you know that. But Philip remains our king. I only wish to be your stadtholder, but together, you and I, we must try to break the powerful yoke of the Duke of Alva. We must get rid of the tyrant and his soldiers. We must fight for freedom. And then we will tell Philip, 'You are, and will remain, our king, but we want to be a free nation — free to worship God in the way we believe He wants to be served and free to retain our old rights and privileges.'"

William of Orange spoke these words in the fall of 1572 to the States of Holland and Zealand. No, he had not sought his own greatness and honour. That was true.

*The king of Spain I've granted*
*My lifelong loyalty.*

During the days of 1572, a new joy lived in the heart of Orange. What had been the cause of that? Driven by hunger and need, the fierce Sea Beggars[1] had unexpectedly captured the city of Briele. The prince had shaken his head in amazement. What good could the pirate's action possibly do? The flag of the prince, of orange, white, and blue, now fluttered from the high tower of the St. Cathrijne Church. This was the first place in the Netherlands that had dared to display this flag. But what good could it possibly do? If Alva would send his Spanish troops . . .

---

[1] The Sea Beggars were people who fled because of their faith.

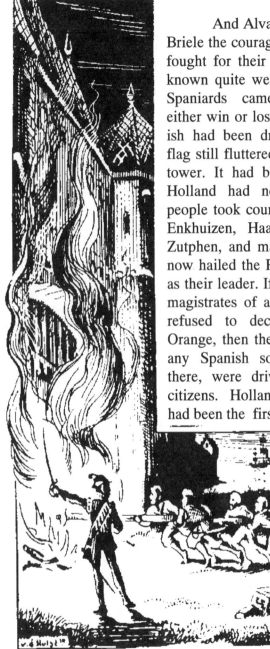

And Alva had done so. In Briele the courageous pirates had fought for their lives. They had known quite well that when the Spaniards came, they would either win or lose. But the Spanish had been driven back. The flag still fluttered proudly on the tower. It had been the miracle Holland had needed, and the people took courage. Vlissingen, Enkhuizen, Haarlem, Alkmaar, Zutphen, and many more towns now hailed the Prince of Orange as their leader. If the mayors and magistrates of a particular town refused to declare loyalty to Orange, then they, together with any Spanish soldiers stationed there, were driven out by the citizens. Holland and Zealand had been the first to stand up for freedom. This had given Orange renewed hope and zeal. *Je maintiendrai*!

*     *     *

It was a dark night. Orange was tired. His body craved rest. He stumbled into his tent and dropped half-undressed to his cot. He lived in the open country now. He was far from Holland and Zealand. With much difficulty he had gathered together another army and had marched to the southern Netherlands[1] close to the French border to assist his brave brother Louis.

Louis had gained entry to the city of Bergen where he now awaited help from France. If the French king, Charles IX, would help drive away the Spanish, and if the Huguenots[2] would also attack the Spanish troops, then . . .

But this was not to be. Instead a horrible thing had happened. Charles IX, who had extended sincere friendship to the Huguenots, had been informed by false sources that the Huguenots were plotting against him. He had given the command to seize and imprison them. In one night, thousands of Huguenots were deceitfully slain. This night has become known as the dreadful St. Bartholomew's Night.

Louis' hope vanished. And worse yet, Spanish troops had sieged the city of Bergen. Louis and his men had been taken as prisoners. For this reason William and his army left Germany. Louis and his companions must be rescued if possible.

---

[1] Today's Belgium.

[2] The French protestants.

Orange's forces approached closer and closer to the Spanish soldiers. How soon would the fighting begin? Tomorrow?

Now, in the dark of night, he lay exhausted, sound asleep. Silence had fallen on the camp. Guards patrolled the perimeter. It was quiet in the tents, but in Orange's tent something stirred. At the prince's feet lay a little dog. He was the prince's faithful companion, that followed wherever his master went and who always slept on his bed.

Troubled, the animal raised his little head. Had he heard something? He pricked up his ears and bared his teeth as though facing a fearsome foe. His eyes looked fiercely at the tent's entrance. Suddenly, the little dog burst into a frenzy of barking. He leaped from the bed and then back onto it. He darted to the door and then back again. It was as though his wild barking called, Master! Master! Wake up! Master, please listen! Don't you hear anything?

But the prince slept peacefully and deeply. The barking became more urgent and more frenzied. Master, wake up! When that did not help, the frantic dog jumped onto his master's chest and scratched his face with his little paws. Master!

Then Orange was forced to wake up. Impatiently and angrily he sought to push the bothersome dog away. But then, wait! He sat up in alarm. Listen! What was that? There, outside the tent. The clatter of weapons, shouting and moaning! Orange leaped from his bed and rushed out of the tent.

The enemy was in the camp! Orange could now see clearly that the guards had been overpowered. His soldiers had been caught unawares while they slept; they were unable to fight. The Spanish soldiers were hurrying toward his tent. He could see that they all wore their vests over their armour so they could recognize each other in the darkness. Then he understood. It was because of him! He was to be captured, dead or alive, and brought to Alva. How pleased that tyrant would be if they found him. But William acted quickly. Through the darkness he ran to the horses tethered beyond the tents. He flung himself onto the first horse and galloped away into the safe, black night. Behind him raced his faithful little dog.

It was a wonder how that animal had saved his master's life. The clever little dog did not realize just how precious that life was. He would have warned his master if he had been but a poor beggar. He had done a good deed. He had spared the Prince of Orange for country and nation. But then, it had not been simply the dog's doing but God's fatherly love which had protected Orange through the actions of this simple animal. Called by God, Orange, helper of the oppressed and persecuted Netherlanders, had not yet finished his work. In the Lord's care he was safe.

The prince returned to Holland. Louis was forced to give up the city of Bergen. He managed to negotiate safe passage for his troops and their weapons. The Spanish had promised this, and they kept their word. However, Louis was sick and was transported in a litter to Dillenburg. Day and night, for many months, Juliana, his loving mother, cared for him. Everyone believed he would die. Would he be the second son to die?

William was worried. It was strange. Sometimes it seemed as if the Lord had swept his carefully made plans right out of his hands. He bowed his head. Through all these trials and afflictions, his faith in God's guidance grew. In his suffering, he knew himself to be a child of his heavenly Father.

## 16. The Secret

It was 1572. Vengeance stalked the land. Alva's soldiers roamed everywhere. All the cities and towns that had dared to declare for the prince were to be punished. The iron grip in which Alva had tried to hold these despicable "people of butter" had to become tougher, more cruel. Was Alva already afraid of how they managed to slip through his fingers?

"Onward! Without pardon!" The rebellious towns were to be punished with fire and sword. Alva's son, Don Frederick de Toledo, was in charge. He was a heartless Spaniard, a cruel son of a cruel father. From Bergen he went to Mechlin[1] and on to Zutphen, Naarden, and so on. Poor cities. They surrendered willingly. They had to, and they hoped for mercy. Mercy from Don Frederick? The slaughter was abominable. As they travelled throughout the land, they left a trail of death and destruction. Farms were burned to the ground, and villages were plundered. Corpses hung from trees or from the rafters of half destroyed houses which had once been peaceful dwellings.

"Onward! Without pardon!" Misery increased. Was there no longer any hope for deliverance? The prince! More than ever the despairing people placed their hope in the prince. Who else in the world was to be trusted? Finally they understood the great love of Orange. He was not concerned for himself; he offered himself.

The prince was coming. But he no longer had an army. He had no money. Small, undisciplined troops of beggars roved about, but that was all. Nevertheless, he was coming. Just as a mother tends to her sick child, unable to take the pain away, unable to help, but sitting at the bedside to comfort and make her child understand that he is safe. So Prince William came, quietly, accompanied by his few supporters across the South Sea to Holland. He knew that he risked his life, but he came anyway.

William wrote to his brother John, "I fear that everyone will forsake me unless God intervenes in a miraculous way. I have decided to go to Holland to assess the state of affairs and if need be, to go to my grave."

The prince arrived at Enkhuizen. The people cheered him wildly, as though he had been sent from heaven. He smiled sadly. William longed to help them, to save them, but what could he do? The old familiar love still burned in his

---

[1] Mechlin is a town in the southern Netherlands situated between Antwerp and Brussels.

heart. He would sacrifice everything . . . *Je maintiendrai*!

In 1573 Haarlem, the largest and strongest city of Holland, fell into the hands of the Spaniards, although the prince had done his best to come to its aid. Ruthlessly, the enemy ravaged the city and moved on to the next city. Don Frederick's army wreaked Alva's vengeance throughout the land.

"Let us give up this struggle. It does not help anyway," the people cried. Life had never been so dark and dismal as in those days.

"Orange, let us surrender! Why should you live in poverty and in constant peril of death? Go back to Germany. Perhaps you will become rich and powerful again. What does this insignificant little country of Holland matter to you? Nothing will help anymore, unless perhaps you know of a powerful friend, a mighty king or emperor who can help you and us."

But the prince answered them calmly and firmly, "Before I took up the cause of defending the Christians and the other oppressed people of these lands, I made a sure alliance with the highest Prince of princes, and I am confident that all who trust in Him will be delivered by His powerful hand in spite of His and our enemies."

Orange's faith in the Lord was firm. Then incredibly, and perhaps even foolishly, the men of Holland and Zealand, an insignificant small number of people living in the low flat country of water and pastures, took courage and persevered. It was only a tiny part of the world, and it seemed ridiculously weak and powerless. Was freedom from Spain, the mightiest country in the world, to be won here? Impossible! And yet it could be done. There was a secret that the Spaniards could never understand. And these cowardly and disheartened, these traitors in the country, and all those in league with the enemy would never understand either.

The secret was the steady, immovable faith of the prince and of his people — the certainty that their cause was honourable and just. They believed it was the will of God to persevere to the end — even to the bitter end. This was the secret of their courage.

Prince William was no longer a Roman Catholic and had not been for a long time. During those dark days, he had joined the confessors of the Reformed faith. Now he was one of them, and his heart was at peace. However fearful and grim the future, the prince would hold fast. *Je maintiendrai*!

It would be the Prince of Orange who would instill courage and trust in the people, in the perilous days ahead. He knew how to keep them united as brothers in danger. Without soldiers and without money, he was the quiet, great leader. And had he deserted them or if a Spanish bullet would have hit its mark, how easily that poor little country would have become spoil for the Spaniards, its people scattered and without hope.

But Orange did not leave, and a Spanish bullet did not kill him. He was safe in the Lord's protection. He had to execute God's plans for the Netherlands.

Philip, Alva, Don Frederick, and all those others hated William with a deep hatred. "Onward! With fire and sword Holland will be humiliated, devastated, and annihilated! And Orange, that stubborn prince, shall bow down! Onward, without pardon!"

## 17. Poor Mother, Poor Prince!

"They have gone! Hurray, our city is free! Away with the Spaniards!" The people of Leiden cheered and celebrated.

It was 1574, and there was reason for great rejoicing. The Spanish soldiers who had surrounded the city, cutting it off from aid and supplies, had abruptly departed. This move was totally unexpected and not at all typical of Spanish strategy. The previous year Don Frederick had suffered a humiliating defeat at Alkmaar. The citizens of Alkmaar had courageously and stubbornly defended their city and, when the prince threatened to flood the surrounding countryside, the Spanish soldiers had been forced to retreat. The fighting had been fierce, but Alkmaar had been saved. The shout had gone up, "Victory has begun at Alkmaar!"

The Spanish then turned to Leiden, a major city and trading centre at that time. But this time Don Frederick did not lead the siege. This was fortunate. Both Don Frederick and his father had returned to Spain. Alva's cruel tyranny had finally come to an end. His cruel plans did not succeed although thousands had been murdered. The "people of butter" had slipped through his fingers. Cursing them, he silently returned to Spain. Another governor came in his stead. Requesens seemed friendlier, but, encouraged by his king, he was to use whatever means necessary to subdue the people. Without exception they were to repent and return to the Roman Catholic Church. This was his most important task.

The first victim of this new governor was the city of Leiden. But strangely, this siege was different from the Spanish sieges in the past. This time the enclosure of the city, with an iron ring of soldiers and cannon, was quiet and relaxed. This was quite different from Don Frederick's strategy. The Spaniards had now become cautious. They knew how bitterly and stubbornly the people of Holland had defended, and would again defend, their city walls when attacked by the enemy. Different tactics were required. The entire city was surrounded so that no one could go in or out. Slowly the city would starve to defeat. But, before all the entrenchments were dug and before all the cannons were set in place, the Spanish left! Why?

Louis and Henry, the prince's brave brothers, who together with William had sacrificed everything for the cause, had recruited an army in Germany. They planned to conquer Brussels! This was the reason the Spanish army had abandoned its siege on Leiden in such haste. Requesens' troops were hurrying to intercept Louis and his men. The two opposing armies met and engaged in battle on the heath outside the tiny village of Mook situated on the Maas River.

Meanwhile, Leiden was free! Prince William immediately sent messengers to the city to urge them to reinforce the city walls and gates without delay and to gather in as much food as possible in case the enemy decided to return. But Leiden did not heed his wise advice. Some of the councillors had already decided to surrender the city if the Spanish came back. They feared the same fate as Haarlem, Naarden, and Zutphen. They did not gather in great quantities of provisions.

The prince left his home in Delft and travelled to Bommel where he met his brothers and their army. These days he travelled a great deal to encourage the people. In Bommel he wrote to his brothers Louis and Henry. He took up his quill and wrote, his brow furrowed with anxiety, "My brothers, since I last wrote to you, I have heard that your foot-soldiers and some of your cavalry have deserted. Has the battle already been lost? March quickly with the remainder of your troops to Emden, and do not come to Holland lest the people become discouraged and lose heart at seeing what has become of your army."

The letter had been sent, but no reply came. Rumours abounded, but no one seemed to know the truth. Three days later Prince William sat at his writing-table again. His dark eyes were fearful, and his hand trembled when he wrote.

"My brothers, I am deeply worried and concerned that I have not yet received any tidings or answer from you. Please send me word immediately!"

Again the letter had been sent, and again there was no response. Oh yes, it was said that Louis and Henry had been miserably defeated. It was also said that the two brothers had been seen with a small party of riders engaged in the heat of battle, attacking the enemy with desperate courage while their cowardly mercenaries had fled. But no one seemed to know more about them . . . It was said that the conquering Spanish army had marched away.

Prince William heard it all. The answer he awaited for never came — would never come. Those days were bitter and sad for William and for the good, gentle old mother far away in Dillenburg. That dreadful uncertainty! Where were the brave and gallant brothers? Had they fled? Were they wounded? Had they been slain?

Yet once again the prince bent over his table, pen in hand. He thought of his mother, his heart filled with compassion for her. She loved her sons so very much. She had cared for them so faithfully. Louis had always carried a small piece of paper hidden in his helmet. On it was a prayer written by his mother. Where was the helmet now? Where was Louis? William's heart broke with intense grief.

"Oh Louis, my brave brother. You have always worked, fought, and suffered for our oppressed people. Have you now also given your life? First Adolf — and now you and Henry? Have three sons been sacrificed? Oh my poor, poor mother!"

But in the letter which he sent to John, his only remaining brother, he had also written the words, "Even if we all have to die, and even if all of the people would be murdered or scattered, we shall always have this assurance — that God will never forsake His own."

No one has ever discovered the mystery of Louis and Henry's deaths. Were they mutilated and trampled by the pounding hooves of warhorses and thrown into a common soldiers' grave? No one knows. There were rumours saying that both men had been severely wounded and dragged into a wooden shack and set on fire. But no one knows for sure, and the true account of their death remains hidden. Louis was thirty-six years old and Henry was twenty-four. Poor mother! Poor prince!

Amazingly William did not lose heart. In the midst of so much calamity and so much adversity he remained strong and steadfast, a true hero.

## 18. Father William

The room was quiet and dark. The fading glow of twilight shone faintly through the tall bow window. It was autumn. Nightfall came early. An elaborately-carved bed stood in the quiet chamber. Its canopy and draperies were dark. One of its curtains had been drawn back.

A man lay in the bed. He tossed restlessly. His face was flushed with fever; his dark eyes scanned the room impatiently. Another man sat beside the bed with pen in hand; a small sheet of paper lay on the writing-table before him. It was very quiet in the room, as it was in the entire house. The building was really an old monastery, sombre and silent.

From the bed came a soft, weak voice. "Write; tell them I always think of them. Tell them I will try everything, risk everything, to help them. But do not tell them how sick I am. It might discourage them."

The writer at the bedside looked at the sick man in profound sorrow and sadly shook his head. Softly he answered, "Yes, Your Highness, I shall take care of it. But rest now. Do not speak anymore. Don't think so much. Your Highness must rest now, sleep, and forget. Those are the doctor's orders."

The sick one smiled. "Forget? Don't think? Don't worry? That is impossible!"

"Your Highness, you must. Your life depends on it."

"Your Highness," the man had said. Who was it who lay ill and feeble in the dark bed in that sombre house? It was Prince William. The man who waited on him was his personal secretary. The other attendants had been dismissed from the house. The prince was afraid his illness might be contagious and wished to spare them. Only two faithful men remained, his secretary and his butler. Day and night they watched over their master and cared for his needs. If only he would rest! Occasionally he dozed fitfully. But in his delirium, he called out orders. They heard his dejected cries.

"The water, the water! If only the water would rise higher!"

What was the cause of this feverish restlessness? What fears plagued his dreams?

Leiden. The plight of that wretched city that had refused to obey tore at his heart. Leiden was once again besieged by Spanish soldiers. Their strong entrenchments encircled the city. They were there to stay, patiently and stubbornly. The siege had forced the inhabitants to make do with the provisions that remained within its walls. It was impossible to get more supplies.

The prince had declared, "I will help them. Leiden must not surrender. Haarlem has fallen. Amsterdam still belongs to the Spanish. If Leiden also falls, then all the largest and strongest cities will again be in the hands of the enemy. Then

Holland and Zealand will be separated. Leiden must hold fast! It must persevere. I shall do everything I can!"

He had helped them. Not with a powerful army — for he had none. Nor did he have the money to wage war. Brothers who might have helped him lay dead, and no one knew where their graves were. And yet he had helped the stricken city. He had written to Leiden. "Hold fast! As long as a man draws breath in this country, we will fight for our freedom and for our faith."

William had written again and again. Far from the besieged city, he had given direction, encouragement, and had promised help.

Help! What could a collection of wild privateers sent out from Zealand, a mere handful of pirates, do against the mighty entrenchments of the enemy? But there was an alliance — a very strange one — and if it would support the prince against the Spanish, then they would be overthrown. Then the enemy itself would be besieged.

In strategic places, the dikes near the entrenched Spanish army had been penetrated. Holes had been dug through these mighty walls that held back the sea. "It was better to have flooded land than lost land!" Now if only the water would rise!

Ships lay at anchor in the vicinity, ready to rescue the citizens of Leiden. The ships were full of Sea Beggars willing to attack the Spaniards, even if they were outnumbered ten to one! But first the water must rise and flood the lowlands. Only a couple of hand's breadth were needed to bring the water pouring in. However, if it did not get any higher, even the flat-bottomed boats would not be able to bring help.

The hunger and misery in Leiden was getting worse and worse. And then the prince became sick — sick unto death. Working day and night, coping with wretchedness and difficulties, had eroded his health. Now he lay in the old, sombre monastery in Rotterdam, far from his family, far from the safety of his home in Germany. He was alone, with only two faithful servants.

The latest report said Leiden was ready to surrender. Perhaps it had already done so. William's doctor advised him to rest, sleep, and forget. But no doctor could purge Orange's heart of his intense love for his people. This was the love which had caused him so much anguish and anxiety and perhaps even his final downfall. In his tortured dreams he had heard the cries of the distraught city calling to him begging for help. Then he had pictured himself upon the lonely dikes where the water refused to burst through, and he would awaken in terror. Oh, Leiden! Were you doomed? Would all of Holland now be doomed? Would all his work, his suffering, his misery be for nothing? Would God allow His people to be overthrown? Was that His will? Those days of anguish and nights of torment were bitter ones for the suffering, sick prince.

Now the fading twilight had turned the darkening room even more sombre. Once again the secretary sat at the table writing a message of encouragement on a small scrap of paper to the citizens of Leiden. Later, this paper would be rolled up and fastened under the wing of a carrier pigeon. The bird, itself, would not realize the task it performed, flying over enemy lines to its nest in Leiden where men would find the message. That is, if all went well and it was not shot down by a Spanish bullet.

The secretary said to himself, "What is the use? Perhaps Leiden will have yielded before it receives this message. Yet, I must and will do my master's will."

Suddenly, the knocker fell against the door with a thud. The prince startled in alarm. A man stood at the door requesting admittance. He carried a message for the prince from Leiden. Risking his life, he slipped through the enemy lines during the dark of night. He came to report that Leiden had not surrendered yet but that sickness and starvation were rampant. The plague had killed hundreds. The people were desperate; yet steadfastly they held the walls, watching, waiting, and suffering. Leiden had not yet fallen.

The prince listened to the news. His eyes lit up. It seemed as though new life flowed through his weakened body. The final fading flickers of evening light gleamed on the dark panelling of the bed-chamber. For Orange, it was as though he had received comfort from heaven. Finally, for the first time since he had fallen ill, he slept peacefully.

It was the beginning of his recovery. The secretary wrote a long letter to John of Nassau, on behalf of the prince. The letter contained these words. "God will provide me with everything that is best for my salvation. He will not give me a burden that is heavier than I can bear."

In the centre of Leiden stood an ancient Roman tower. From the top of this tower, starving people searched the distance for help and deliverance. They could no longer tolerate the agony. The horrible plague lurked everywhere. Vicious hunger made them writhe in pain. It became so bad that, whenever they saw him in front of the city-hall on the Breedstraat, they screamed at Peter Adriaanz van den Berg, a city councillor who was against surrendering the city, "Give up the city before we all die!"

The faithful man had staunchly replied, "Never! I will save the city for the prince for as long as I live. But if my body will relieve your hunger, then take it!"

He had drawn his sword and offered it to the people. "Here, kill me, but surrender the city? Never!"

Ashamed, the people had backed away — shamed by such great courage and such true loyalty.

Then, one day at the end of September, gladness and hope lit up the weary faces. A pigeon had delivered the message, "The prince is recovering from his illness. He is coming to look at the dikes."

The people craned their necks to look over the high city walls. If only they could see Orange. Would he be there beyond the enemy entrenchments far in the distance? They longed for him.

The prince of Orange did come. He came to see the faithful Sea Beggars who waited on every available ship to attack the Spaniards as soon the water was high enough. He came to instill courage and patience. In the grey distance, for it was fall, he saw the afflicted city. If only the water would rise. If only it would not be too late and the city would be forced to surrender. Disheartened and discouraged, he returned to Delft where he now lived.

*       *       *

A week later, on a Sunday afternoon, the prince had gone to church. He sat in his pew listening attentively, but his face was grave, his eyes dark with worry and sorrow. There was total silence in the church. The only sound was the minister's voice.

Suddenly, strangely, a voice called outside the door. Right in the middle of the church service, a man rushed into the church! He was covered with dust and sweat; his hair stuck out in all directions. In one hand he held a letter — in the other his riding whip. Breathless and panting, he gazed around the church.

"The prince! Where is the prince?" he whispered impatiently.

"There, there in the high pew," someone pointed.

He hurried to the prince. He could not wait for the service to be finished. He had ridden as a wild man. He held out the letter.

Orange had heard the noise and watched the man approach his pew. A letter? And why was the man so impatient? Why were his eyes shining? Could he not wait until the worship service had ended? But the prince took the letter and read it. His frail hand quivered; his pale face flushed with joy. Folding his hands, he offered thanks to God. The letter was given to the minister who read it aloud. "Leiden has been liberated! Leiden is free!"

What a strange, wonderful worship service! When it was over, the messenger, who had ridden his horse in one stretch from Leiden to Delft, told the whole story. The water had risen. The Sea Beggars had drawn nearer, but a strong enemy force had held them back. Then, without warning, on Saturday night, a section of the city wall had caved in. It had caused a dreadful fright. That very same night, the Spaniards, afraid of the menacing flood of water, slipped away! A starving young boy had been the first to venture outside the city. In the abandoned trenches he had found a delicious stew!

Leiden was saved! Bringing all kinds of food, the Beggars had sailed down the canals into the city, amid loud cheers and rejoicing.

The next day . . .

"Your Highness, do not go to the city. It is too dangerous. You are not yet well, and the plague is still about."

"I will go," insisted Orange. "I must shake hands with those brave, gallant men. Those fine, wonderful men and women and those poor, starving children have saved Holland through their unselfish perseverance with God's help."

When the prince arrived in Leiden, the crowds thronged to see him, to hear him. They wanted to express their thanks with words and hands. Their sparkling eyes showed how much they cared for him.

"Father William! Father William!" they shouted. He had earned that name.

*　　　*　　　*

As a reward for courage and endurance, a university was established in the city of Leiden. It was the first academy in Holland where young men could receive training for the ministry.

## 19. A Wonderful Day

Problems, serious problems! William of Orange's life was filled with difficulties. Again and again he faced misfortune and sorrow. Yet, with his whole heart, he trusted in God's loving care. Regardless of the problems, his motto remained *Je maintiendrai*! Despite his difficulties, he remained friendly to rich and poor, whether a wealthy heir or a crude Sea Beggar. He could laugh and jest, be cheerful and thankful. But in his heart there remained a deep sorrow for the plight of his people. By 1576, two years after the liberation of Leiden, William sank to the depths of despair. The bitter struggle with the Spaniards had continued. The war was costly, and the impoverished people had no money left. The Prince of Orange, his mother, and his brother John also had no money. Everything had been offered and given. No other country offered to help: not Germany, nor France, nor England. That small, ravished country of Holland and Zealand had had to remain steadfast and strong on its own. Perhaps if Orange had not supported them, the struggle would have been given up long ago.

But then, in 1576, Zierikzee, the bridge of land which joined Holland and Zealand, fell into Spanish hands. Orange's spirit failed. He shook his head in discouragement when he heard the sad news. The plan he thought of was born of desperation and despair.

"Let us give up the struggle," he said, "It is hopeless. Let us gather all the seagoing ships and take on board all the men, women, and children who have refused to give up their freedom and their worship and cross the great sea to find a new homeland. We will destroy our windmills and our dikes, burn our towns and villages, and give our country back to the sea. It is better to lose one's country than to lose one's freedom."

It was a desperate plan, but pressure and distress made

the usually calm prince sick at heart.

Then, strangely and unexpectedly, deliverance came! Requesens, the governor who had taken Alva's place in 1573, died. The Spanish soldiers who had not received pay for their services for a long time, mutinied. In great numbers they withdrew to the south where many people had remained Roman Catholic and had not seen much fighting. The large, wealthy cities of Antwerp and Brussels would provide riches and plunder for the rebellious Spaniards.

Those poor cities, overrun by ruthless, merciless, mutineers! Antwerp, a prosperous city of trade and commerce, was ransacked and the people were brutally tortured or killed and stripped of all their possessions. Even the Roman churches, with the likeness of Mary embroidered on their banners and flags, were vandalized and plundered by Roman Catholic Spaniards, in a manner many times worse than during the terrible image-breaking wave of 1566.

So it was that the southern provinces cried out to William of Orange for help and deliverance from the Spanish mobs. How did he answer them? Did he refuse and remind them that they had not aided Holland and Zealand in their time of need? No. Their cry for help had made his heart leap for joy. That day was certainly one of the best of his life! Of course he would go. Of course he would help. This was how it should be. At last, all the provinces were to be united against Spain. This had always been his secret desire — that everyone, Romanists and non-Romanists, would live together as one nation and would fight together for freedom as one nation! Now, suddenly, the opportunity had come!

In the town of Ghent an agreement was drawn up between the northern and southern provinces. The Pacification of Ghent was written under the direction of William of Orange. It was a wonderful time of his life!

In Brussels there was great celebrating and rejoicing.

Bells rang, clocks chimed, and cannons were fired. The people paraded in the streets and shouted, "He is coming! He is really coming!"

Four thousand armed men escorted Orange through the streets of the city. All the leading nobles were included in the splendid procession that surrounded him. The people cheered and jostled to get a better view. They wanted to tell him that they had not forgotten their prince, and that their love for him was still alive.

"Orange! Orange!"

It was the year 1577. Ten years ago Alva had come. Ten years ago William of Orange had fled from Brussels, a fugitive. Now, as a returning prince, he made a triumphant entry into his own city. William had returned. His heart overflowed with joy — not at receiving all the glory and honour, for he could have had those in a far easier manner, if he had so desired — but he was glad that the struggle against Philip's tyranny had not been for nothing.

William rode through the market square. The trumpets sounded, the flags waved, and the people cheered. In this same square, Egmond and Horne had died on the scaffold. He saw the palace where Margaret, the governess, had lived and where his brother Louis had delivered the Petition of the Noblemen to her. If only Louis could have been here!

Two days later Prince William swore an oath of allegiance before a great assembly of people in the city. He pledged allegiance to them all — a united people.

That night, William of Orange slept in a palace in Brussels. His own former palace had been ransacked in obedience to Alva's orders. He remembered the happy days of his youth and all the glamour and glory of that time. He thought of the great misfortunes which had befallen him later. But he also thought, I have never regretted it. I believe that it was God's will to sacrifice everything for the freedom of my beloved people. I have done so out of love. If only everything would be well now. Surely it is possible for Roman Catholics and Protestants to live together in harmony as neighbors. I, myself, have also bidden farewell to the Roman church. I desire the freedom to serve God according to His Word, but that does not make me an enemy of the Romanists!"

Once again William slept in the old city where, years earlier as a young boy, eleven years old, he had gone to join the imperial household of Charles V. Now he was forty-four years old but looked much older. His hair was grey, furrows lined his forehead, and lines of fatigue framed his mouth. Trials and worries had aged him. Yet that night he slept as the acclaimed leader of the people of the Netherlands, and his own city had welcomed him back.

However, the unity of the Netherlands did not last long. The prince's beautiful dream of a united people, Roman Catholics and Protestants, was quickly shattered. The people simply could not understand the depth and sincerity of the prince's heart. A hundred years would pass before his dream would be possible.

Today people of many religions live together in harmony under one government in one country. All share the same rights and privileges. Prince William had thought it possible in his time. But by some he was considered a fool; others thought him reckless or a hypocrite; and still others felt he was a godless man without religion or beliefs. He was greatly misunderstood.

It did not take long before the southern provinces came to an agreement with each other. This was known as the Union of Arras. Fear of the Spanish soldiers had lessened. Again the southern provinces had promised King Philip their allegiance and the restriction of worship to the Roman Catholic religion. William was dismayed. He had worked hard to unite the northern and southern provinces but had failed. The Pacification of Ghent had been broken. Now he feared for Holland and Zealand. Once again that small nation had been abandoned. New dangers threatened them. But, *Je maintiendrai*!

A few weeks later, on January 23, 1579, the northern provinces drew up an agreement known as the Union of Utrecht. Prince William worded the agreement, but his brother, John of Nassau, made the arrangements. Even then William had wished to make it clear that he favoured a union of all the people, undivided by religious beliefs and prejudices. But the lands of the south had once again bowed beneath the yoke of the Spanish tyrant, while the lands of the north continued with the struggle for freedom.

"With our possessions and our lives, we shall support each other!" These words had been written in the articles of the Union of Utrecht. John of Nassau had spoken them before a solemn assembly.

The seven northern provinces continued the struggle alone for another seventy years. But no one, not even the Prince of Orange, realized that beforehand.

\*     \*     \*

A great blessing and source of happiness for the prince was his wife, Charlotte of Bourbon. She understood him, cared for his needs, and provided him with a safe, comfortable home where he could lay his troubles aside for a while. She was a source of friendship and sunny happiness, in an often dark and bitter world.

## 20. "I Dedicate Undying Faith to This Land of Mine"

Enemies of the Prince of Orange were to be found everywhere. They were not only Spaniards but also Netherlanders, sons of the people he fought and suffered for. Many were envious noblemen who begrudged the prince's great love for his people. There were also ignorant people, unable to understand the true purpose of his endeavors. Then there were the traitors among the people, who eagerly accepted money from the Spanish for falsely accusing William of all kinds of evil. Yes, the prince had many enemies, and their hatred, envy, and treachery often caused much bitterness in his life. Nevertheless he held his head high, the light of faithfulness to his beliefs and to his people shining in his eyes.

A meeting had been called — a very dignified assembly of the country's leaders. Prince William as stadtholder was also present, in the place of honour. They came to discuss the distress and persecution of their people. The city of Maestricht had been overtaken by the Spaniards and many of its inhabitants were brutally murdered. But now King Philip sent a delegation to the Netherlands on a mission of peace. Could he be serious?

During the meeting a messenger entered the chamber bearing a letter addressed to the States-General. He gave it to the official clerk who began to read it aloud to the assembly. First he read one sentence, then another, and another. But then he faltered and began to stutter. Finally he stopped altogether, too afraid to continue.

"Yes, stop, do not read on!" shouted the listeners who had immediately recognized the slander and lies it contained, defaming the prince.

Prince William took the letter. What would he do with

it? Would he destroy it in anger because of the treachery it
contained, or would he insist that its contents were but ugly lies
and trample it under foot? He did none of these, but held his
head high, the light of faithfulness shining in his eyes, and
calmly and clearly read the letter aloud. It stated that it had
been his fault that Maestricht had fallen to the enemy. He was
to blame for the loss of the thousands of men, women, and
children who had been so ruthlessly slaughtered. He was the
cause of King Philip's fierce anger against his subjects. It was
totally the prince's fault that there was no peace in the land and
that if he were gone . . .

All this William read aloud. When he had finished, he placed the letter on the table and gazed at the honest and sincere faces of the men before him. They jumped to their feet in anger, their fists clenched and their eyes flaming with indignation and protest against the injustice of the traitor who had dared write these slanderous lies. The prince, alone, remained calm and composed.

He said, "I have done the best I could, but if you want me to go, then I will do so. I belong to my people with all my heart, but if you ask me not to continue in the struggle for the freedom of the Netherlands, then I will do as you wish."

"No, no!" shouted the men. "Away with the slander!"

They surrounded him, cheering for him, telling him with their words, their gestures, and their eyes, of their loyalty and trust. No slander would ever rob him of their love. Orange was filled with gratitude. The false poison of the letter had failed. Everything had worked for the better. Orange and his people had been drawn closer.

In Cologne the Spanish delegates had met with some of the leaders of the provinces who formed the Union of Utrecht. "Peace, we have come to seek peace," proclaimed the Spanish.

"We also desire peace," agreed the Netherlanders.

But peace could not be achieved. King Philip was willing to forgive and forget everything except freedom of religion for his subjects. That would be impossible, for he feared the wrath of God for such a great sin. On the other hand the Netherlanders, who had already fought for more than ten years, offering possessions and blood, life and happiness for exactly that same freedom of religion, were willing to accept King Philip as their sovereign. But they would not return to the Roman Catholic church, for they knew that then they would sin greatly against God. No, there could not be peace!

The Spanish had another suggestion. If only Orange would leave the country! He was the leader of the rebellious people. He had stirred them up to rise against their king. He had to go. Then the farmers and fishermen of these lowlands would submit to the king, and Philip would have his wish. Orange must disappear! Secretly and cunningly, the Spanish delegates sent a list of tempting promises to the prince.

"Do you wish to become wealthy again? You are so poor now," they asked. "The king is willing to give you vast sums of money so you can live as a great prince again. He will return your estates and castles that he confiscated in the Netherlands. Then he will return your son, Philip William, who still remains in Spain. All this he will do, if you promise to leave Holland and leave the people to their own fate. Why would you not do this? Why would you choose to be poor, with so many worries? Why would you continue to suffer and live in great danger? Leave those people alone, and you will be happy!"

The crafty delegates had worded their promises carefully. They firmly believed that William would accept their proposals. Surely his heart longed for his son. Certainly he would prefer riches and honour over poverty and misery. But they were foolish men. They did not know the noble heart of Orange.

William dealt scornfully with their sly promises. He answered, "Neither for money or goods, nor for the sake of my own life, nor for my wife or children will I mix one drop of this traitorous poison in my cup! These my people and I have begun this perilous struggle together — and together, with the strength God will give, we will persevere. Je maintiendrai!"

The plan had failed! Orange would never forsake or betray his people.

*William of Nassau, scion*
*Sprung of an ancient line,*
*I dedicate undying*
*Faith to this land of mine.*

## 21. Tranquil Amid the Angry Waves

A year later, in 1580, a great shock rent the land.

"Traitor! Is that a true king — our king? How dare he? This is terrible!"

In fear and anger the people read the messages sent by King Philip. Again and again they read them, for they could scarcely believe their eyes. But the words were clear and simple. Their eyes blazed with anger; their hearts were filled with abhorrence.

"Assassin!"

What caused this outcry against this tyrant who was in Spain and schemed his hellish plans? This time the king had pronounced a ban against the Prince of Orange. This was dreadful. Prince William had been declared an outlaw, a hunted man, exiled from every country in the world. No place would be safe for him. No one was allowed to invite him into their home for food, drink, or to provide him with shelter. No one was permitted to be his friend. He was banned, to be hunted as a wild animal. He was to be killed as a terrible criminal.

Philip had written, "Orange, accursed hypocrite, is the cause of all the misery suffered by the people of the lowlands. He is a liar, a Judas, an enemy of the human race. Anyone having the courage to deliver us from this wicked will . . ."

But who would dare kill Orange? The people shuddered when they read the edict or heard it discussed. The person who succeeded in killing the prince would receive twenty-five thousand crowns in gold from King Philip, as well as forgiveness for any crimes he might have committed. Furthermore, if he were not already a member of the nobility, he would receive a document ranking him as a noble. If he himself died in the execution of his despicable deed, the promised rewards would be passed on to his heirs.

Traitor! Assassin! Base villain! Was that a true king? Was he really their king? At first Philip had tried to bribe the prince with promises of great wealth if he would just desert them. That had failed. And now Orange was forced to leave. Now he was to die.

Fear and compassion for their prince filled the hearts of his people. They were determined to fight for him and protect him; they realized only too clearly the great danger he was in. They also realized that a greedy assassin would work cunningly, and who would know when he would strike?

Certainly, thousands of fervent prayers for the safety of the prince were sent up daily all over the Netherlands. In splendid castles, in peasant huts, in stately merchants' homes, in cities, and in farmhouses, the people beseeched God for William's protection. Father William! Never had the people loved him as much as now.

Prince William had also read the pronouncement of his banishment. With head held high, he had read it calmly, but his heart ached. Death? No he did not fear death. Thus far he had given everything for the freedom of his people; he would also willingly give his life, if that was necessary. However, Philip's lies and treachery wounded his soul. With the help of some friends, William wrote a letter, a document of defense. He addressed it to the heads of government, but it was meant for all the people to read. Everyone must know — had the right to know what his thoughts were. Sharp words were written against Philip, the tyrant, the man without compassion.

"The calamity this people has suffered is a result of the cruelty and arrogance of the Spaniards, who think to make us slaves as the Indians and Italians are. We are a nation that has never been conquered!"

The letter also contained kind, loving words. These were meant for the people he loved.

"Have I helped you so that I could become rich,

important, and happy? Why have I sacrificed everything — even my brothers, Adolf, Louis, and Henry, who were more dear to me than my own life, and my son who has been abducted and taken to Spain? Why have I placed my own life in jeopardy day and night? It was because I longed to win your freedom! If you think that my death will be of service to you, then I am ready to die. No prince or tyrant will dispose of my head, for I have surrendered it to you. However, if you are of the opinion that I am still able to help you, then let us together persevere in this fearful struggle, united in heart and will. Through the goodness of our God we shall with His blessing defend our people. He has supported me throughout so many times of depression and anxiety. All together, let us save your wives and children as well as everything else which is precious to you. Je maintiendrai, Nassau!"

*     *     *

A painting has been preserved from the days of William of Orange. It is a picture of a wild and tempestuous sea dotted with icebergs. But in the midst of the turbulence and billowing waves, there calmly floats a bird's nest. Upon the nest sits a bird with an orange-brown breast and Nassau-blue feathers. The bird rests there peacefully and contently. A beautiful Latin motto has been inscribed beneath the painting. It reads *Saevis tranquillus in undis*.[1]

As peacefully as the bird rested amid the fierce and stormy waves, William of Orange also remained calm during those days of tumult and strife. He was calm and dignified; his eyes were steady and trusting. The conflict of joy and sorrow, victory and defeat, love and hate, surrounded him in endless

---

[1] Calm amid the raging billows.

turmoil, yet he remained steadfast and at peace. His motto was "Calm amid the raging billows."

The people of the Netherlands loved their prince deeply. Their government did something which a people, a nation, had never done before. They revoked their allegiance to Philip, king of Spain. They simply could no longer be obedient to such a king: an oppressor, an assassin, a cruel man without a heart. King Philip, father of this country? His people had intended to obey him as they had his father, Charles. They had wanted to be his faithful subjects, but he only tried to humiliate them and hold them in slavery. He had impoverished, beaten, tortured, and killed them. He had tried to force them away from God, when they had tried to obey God before men. And then he had sent assassins to rob them of their best — their most faithful friend. No, he could no longer be their "father."

Orange was a true father. He was the father of the "Fatherland." The renunciation of Philip as their king was the bold and courageous reply to the ban issued against William. Now Orange could become their true Prince. William, himself, did not wish for that, for he did not seek his own honour and glory. Considering the plight of his people and the perilous times, he felt they needed the help of a mighty ruler. He arranged for the brother of the king of France to become Lord of the Netherlands. This man was Philip of Anjou. But this Frenchman, a dishonest person, was their leader in name only. The people continued to look upon Prince William as the real Father of the Fatherland. They knew that he was the only one they could trust without doubt.

*The signature of William of Nassau*[1]

---

[1] The prince often wrote in French where he is known as Guillaume de Nassau.

## 22. For the Sake of Money

It was a dark evening. A lone monk hurried down the quiet and deserted streets of Antwerp. Furtively he kept close to the houses that lined the road. When he reached a tall, imposing banker's mansion, he stopped and looked around. Satisfied, he cautiously raised the knocker on the heavy door, and let it fall. The door opened quickly. He was expected.

Inside, the blinds had been drawn. Three men sat in a gloomy room dimly lit by a single candle. They were d'Anastro the banker, Venero his cashier, and a half-witted clerk Jean Jauregui. All three men were Spanish and worked in Antwerp. D'Anastro's eyes were filled with tears, as he peered stealthily at the clerk who was praying with bowed head.

At one time d'Anastro had been a wealthy man. Now he was unable to pay his debts and was on the verge of bankruptcy. He would have to leave Antwerp. That was a shame! But there was hope. There was a way to get money. Together with Venero, he had worked out a plan; Jean Jauregui, a fanatical fool, would carry it out. Everything was ready, Jauregui was prepared. Only one thing was lacking, but the monk Timmerman would take care of that.

The knocker thudded on the outside door. Timmerman had arrived. In the eerie gloom the half-witted clerk knelt before the monk. His face was pale, and his hands trembled with nervousness. What did he have to fear? This holy father had come to still his fears, had he not? The monk hesitated. What was required of him? Was he to lay his hand on the clerk's head and pronounce the sacred blessing? Was he to pardon the man's sins — including the dangerous act he was about to commit? Evidently this was what the half-wit expected. But Jean Jauregui's heart was not at ease. He was not doing it for the money, at least that was not the most important reason. He was about to perform a noble, God-pleasing deed. If that were only true.

Still the monk hesitated. No, he dare not give absolution.[1] It was his duty to persuade him not to carry out this plan. Jauregui was disappointed.

At the table the other two men sat whispering together in the flickering candlelight. With their heads close together, d'Anastro and Venero were dividing up the wealth, ninety thousand ducats, which the clerk would earn for them. Of course Jean Jauregui would also receive some, but not much, for that was not necessary.

Jean sat alone in the semi-darkness. Carefully he placed his worldly treasures on the bench beside him. They consisted

---

[1] Forgiveness of sins.

of an Agnus Dei,[1] a copy of the catechism written by the Jesuit priests, a sacred candle from the church, a charmed toad skin, a pistol, and a sheathless dagger. Slowly, carefully, he hid them all under his clothes. These sacred items should be enough to guard him from all danger.

The next day was Sunday. It was also a feast day. The Duke of Anjou, brother to the French king, and the man who was to be the new head of state in the Netherlands in Philip's stead, was celebrating his birthday. That evening, William of Orange was to attend the duke's feast. William had gone to church and then had dinner with several French noblemen and with his wife, Charlotte of Bourbon. The meal had ended. Laughing and joking, the prince prepared to leave the dining hall. A man came forward, his head bowed in supplication, his hands trembling. Strangers often entered the prince's palace. The guards had stopped him, but when he had explained that he wished to present a petition to Orange, they allowed him to enter. Orange disliked refusing a petitioner, and his guards knew it. The pale-faced young man gave his letter to the prince. William bent his head to read it.

Then, a shot rang out. Quickly, the man had aimed a pistol at the prince's head and fired! Immediately swords were unsheathed, voices called out, and hands seized, but it was too late. Hit in the neck by the bullet, the prince sank into the arms of his friends.

"Don't kill him," he whispered, "I forgive him for causing my death."

His words came too late. Two French noblemen had already pierced Jean Jauregui with their swords. He lay dead.

The unconscious prince was taken to his room where the doctor quickly examined him. William was in critical

---

[1] Agnus Dei means "Lamb of God." It was a medallion with a lamb and a banner inscribed on one side and a picture of a saint on the other.

condition. His faithful wife, Charlotte of Bourbon, who loved her husband so deeply, had collapsed in shock. This was dangerous, for she was a frail woman. In an instant her happy, friendly home had been plunged into mourning.

Down in the dining hall the murderer lay dead. A fifteen-year old boy gazed down at him. The boy's fists were clenched; his eyes filled with tears. He bit his lips hard to keep from crying out, Father, my beloved Father!

That evil man who lay at his feet had murdered his father. Who was he? No one knew.

"Search his pockets," commanded the youth.

Men hurried to obey. The young boy was Prince Maurice, son of Orange. Once again the treasures hidden in Jean Jauregui's clothing appeared: the Agnus Dei, the catechism, the sacred candle, the magic toad skin, all the possessions which had not saved the life of the superstitious half-witted fanatic. Inside his stocking they found a naked dagger. Someone also discovered some letters and a sum of money. His pathetic body was then carried away.

What then of the other two — those villains who had

persuaded the clerk to murder the prince? D'Anastro with his false tears, d'Anastro most cunning of all — had fled across the border to the army of Parma, the Spanish governor.[1] Venero and the monk Timmerman, who had both helped in the plot to assassinate the prince, were captured and condemned to death. It was 1582 — two years after the proclamation of the ban against the Prince of Orange.

In the prince's palace the atmosphere was heavy with sorrow, worry, and fear. The same was true of Antwerp and of the whole country. People gathered in front of the palace and in the streets to hear whatever news they could, although they feared the worst. Day after day Prince William hovered on the brink of death. The wound had bled profusely. The most distinguished doctors in the country attended him. His good wife cared for him with all the love in her heart, forgetting her own weaknesses. Everyone was helpful and fearful. William lay powerless but calm and resigned in submission to the will of God.

The wound healed very slowly, but the hope that the prince would recover grew. Then, suddenly, the wound in his neck broke open, and the bleeding started anew. This was very dangerous because the wound could not be dressed. The tight bandages would cut off his breathing, and yet without them he would slowly bleed to death. Finally it seemed as though the end had come.

"It is over for me," the prince said softly. "If it pleases God, in whose hands I am, to take me to Himself, then I submit with patience to His will. I place my trust in His grace. His mercy alone is my salvation."

However, the Lord's will was different. Prince William's hour had not yet come. One of the doctors had thought

---

[1] After Requesens' death, the Duke of Parma, a son of Margaret of Parma had become the Spanish governor.

of a simple way to stop the dangerous bleeding. The gentle pressure of a finger on a small lead bullet in the hole would prevent the artery from bleeding, until it was healed. This was done. Day and night, week after week, the doctors took turns in this task of love. It worked! The wound healed completely. The evil plan to kill the prince for money had failed. A month after the attempt on his life, Prince William rode to church. It was only fitting that his first outing would be to the house of the Lord where the prince could sincerely thank God in the presence of his people.

The people flocked together to catch a glimpse of their beloved prince. They pushed and shoved to get close to him. Joy and gratitude filled their hearts, and, when they saw him in the crowded church, tears of happiness shone in their eyes. How they loved him.

However, a shadow marred that joy. Charlotte of Bourbon had been unable to accompany her husband. She was very ill. The care, the worry, and the sadness of those dark days had undermined her weak body. Three days later the prince stood weeping at her deathbed. Thus, the murdering lead of Jean Jauregui had indeed destroyed one precious life.

\*      \*      \*

One person had been spared the misery and sorrow of those dark days. Juliana of Stolberg, Orange's faithful mother, had passed from her sad earthly life into the joy of her Lord in 1580, the year of the ban. Her life had been one of suffering and sacrifice, but her generous heart, full of love, had endured it all. Such a mother could have such a son!

## 23. Everything Offered, Everything Sacrificed

It was a beautiful, early Sunday morning in midsummer 1584. A lone man walked beside a quiet canal in the little town of Delft. The beauty of the linden trees were mirrored in the calm water. The man was short. His long coat, old and drab, hung around his ankles. A floppy, brimmed hat was pulled down low, covering his face. Looking out from beneath the brim, the eyes glittered darkly. He crossed a narrow alley, followed a stone wall, and halted at a small gate.

He hesitated for a moment then muttered, "Go on, don't hesitate now." His lips curled briefly in a sneer. Pulling his hat down lower, he bowed his head and passed through the gate. He came upon a small open space in front of a wide, low house with many tiny windows. A few stone steps led up to a very plain door. "Stop," boomed a deep voice. A guard ordered the early morning visitor to remain standing.

The visitor was not afraid. He had been here many times before. With a flourish he swept off his hat and produced some papers from his pocket saying, "Letters for His Highness, the Prince of Orange. May I enter?"

"Wait a moment", ordered the guard, and he disappeared inside the house. He returned quickly and nodded. The bearer of letters was to be allowed in. In the foyer he was met by a servant who took the letters and went to bring them to the prince.

The small man in his long coat, his dark eyes gleaming, waited.

Did the Prince of Orange really live there, in that old monastery of Saint Agatha with its hollow, empty rooms and long, dark halls? Was this a palace for a prince? It was quite different from the magnificent Palace of Nassau in Brussels, where as a boy William had lived amid such pomp and splendour. It was also quite different from that stately castle, Dillenburg. Had Orange become so poor? Poor he was, for he had sacrificed all his worldly riches for his people. However, he was happy and content in the knowledge that he was God's child. His heart was at peace. What did poverty, worry, and danger matter to him? From Antwerp he had moved to the little town of Delft where it was quieter and safer.

Hired rogues lurked constantly near him, seeking his life. Since the wicked, but failed, attempt by Jean Jauregui, four more plots against the prince's life had been discovered. Here in this quiet town beside the tranquil canal, in this old house that had been renamed Prinsenhof,[1] William could continue his work for the care of his people and country. From his large workroom, he sent his letters and messengers out into the world, bearing his wisdom and his love.

William had remarried. His wife was Louise de Coligny. Their six-month old son, Frederick Henry, slept in a cradle. The Prince of Orange lived quietly and peacefully. Only a few guards stood watch over his house and his life. He realized that he was constantly in danger, yet he was at ease and undisturbed — a hero who did not fear death.

In the foyer the man stood waiting. Suddenly word came that he was to go to the prince. Go to the prince? He, himself, was to see the prince! Shaken, the blood rushed to his head. His hand rubbed his coat, searching. What a pity, a real pity, he thought. However, he bowed and meekly followed the servant who escorted him to see the prince in his bedchamber.

William of Orange had not yet risen. He lay in his bed reading the letters that bore the news that Philip of Anjou had suddenly died in Paris. The brother of the King of France was to have been the new governor of the Netherlands. He had been

---

[1] The Court of the Prince.

a wicked and treacherous man. Now the prince wished to see the bearer of these tidings and question him further concerning the matter.

The man drew near and bowed, very humbly and very respectfully. With head lowered he stood before the bed. He was alone with the prince. If only he had a pistol, or a sword, or any weapon. It was too bad! Regret pained his heart. Now he had to stand and answer the prince's questions.

The prince was not thinking of danger at all. The man who stood at his bedside was Francois Guion, a pious Frenchman who had been persecuted for his belief in the Reformed teachings and been banned from his homeland. He had been at Prinsenhof before, but the prince had always sent him to France with letters. He had been a good and faithful messenger. No, the prince was not thinking of danger. Once again the man left the prince and bowed and bowed . . .

Oh, but regret was bitter. If only he had known that he would be escorted to the prince's bedside. He sauntered across the open square in front of the house. His floppy hat was pulled down low, covering his eyes, hiding the false smile which played upon his lips. He thought of Orange, the rebel, wicked enemy of the holy Roman church. The prince was a traitor! If he but knew the danger he had faced that morning. He would not have stayed in bed so trustingly or been so friendly. But the prince had not known. He believed his morning visitor to have been Francois Guion, a heretic and a faithful servant. But he had been deceived. His guest had been Balthasar Gerards. He, Balthasar, was not a heretic; he abhorred heretics, and he especially abhorred the prince. He hated the Prince of Orange with all his heart. To kill him and deliver the world from that pest would be the highest honour of his life.

"I swear that I will do it! Patience — patience and cunning is what I must have. And I will deceive; I will continue to go to the accursed church of the heretics. Pray — I must pray and carry a Bible. But the day will come — and if I must lose my life, it does not matter, as long as that accursed heretic is gone, is dead. Oh, then there will be joy in heaven!"

A sergeant of the guard had seen the man loitering beside the house. Sternly he called, "Why are you walking around here?"

The voice had disturbed Balthasar Gerards' thoughts. But his tongue was glib, and he could be so very friendly. He could also easily rouse compassion. Sadly he shook his head and pointed to his worn stockings and to his shoes.

"I long to go to the Old Church across the street on this beautiful Sunday morning, just as all good people do, but I cannot go like this. I am ashamed to go to church dressed so shabbily, but I do not have any money to buy new shoes and stockings."

The sergeant, a good man at heart, felt sympathy for the poor man. He was not suspicious at all. Although he, himself, could not give the pious Frenchman any money, he promised to plead on his behalf. That same day he spoke to the prince's steward about the pious man who dared not go to church dressed in his shabby clothes. The steward spoke to William, and that very day Balthasar Gerards received money from the prince's own purse.

When Balthasar heard the coins jingling in his pocket, his heart leaped for joy. He had told Parma, the Spanish governor, of his evil plan and asked for money to buy good weapons. Parma had refused, thinking that the proposed attempt on the prince's life was too vile. But now Orange himself had supplied the necessary money. Now he must be patient!

On Monday he bought two pistols as well as some bullets from one of the soldiers of the guard. He was sly and knew just how to talk to the soldier. He even argued about the bullets which he later rubbed with poison. Who would ever guess that the pious little man was a cunning assassin? ·

On Tuesday, July 10, 1584, Balthasar Gerards presented himself at Prinsenhof. He wanted to go to France but needed a passport of proof that he was in the service of the Prince of Orange. He was admitted to the house. No one distrusted him. All the guards knew him well. He waited in the foyer, and before long the prince appeared from his workroom. William was dressed in a long gown, a tabard.[1] His wife accompanied him, for it was noon, time for the family's dinner. They walked together, arms linked, talking and laughing cheerfully with some men who had come to join them. Dinner time was a restful time of the day. The prince would set aside his cares and worries and concentrate on entertaining his family and guests. Later there would be many more hours of work, of pondering and arranging, of dispatching letters and receiving messengers. From his large but plain workroom, he governed his country.

But now it was time for dinner. The dining hall was across from the foyer. A man stood waiting there. When the prince approached, he respectfully removed his hat and bowed — and bowed again. Then, very humbly, he asked the prince for a passport. Orange stopped and listened unsuspectingly. Who would distrust this humble man with his head bowed? But there was one who did not like the looks of him. Louise de Coligny, Orange's wife, had caught a glimpse of his eyes. She shivered uncontrollably and gripped her husband's arm without realizing it. She heard the prince tell the man to return after dinner, and instinctively she pressed closer as though protecting him from some unknown, mysterious danger. She whispered, "Oh, what a disagreeable face he has. His eyes make me shudder!"

---

[1] The prince's tabard is still on display in the Prinsenhof Museum in Delft.

But Prince William laughed gaily at her anxiety. "Oh no! He is Francois Guion, a quiet and pious man. He is a good messenger." William did not know fear.

Balthasar Gerards hurried along the canal that sunny summer afternoon. "At last, the time has come," he muttered. The light of false joy burned in his fierce, dark eyes. For years he had harboured the plan of killing the Prince of Orange, the enemy of the holy Roman church. Once the world was rid of that rebel, the Roman church would be powerful again. A Roman priest, a Jesuit, had already pardoned him for the atrocity he was about to commit. He need fear nothing. In heaven there would be great rejoicing. The hour had finally come. These were the thoughts of a half-crazed fanatic.

At the Diamond Inn, a shabby tavern, everything was silent with the quiet of midday. In secret, Balthasar loaded his pistols. When he judged that the prince's noonday meal would have ended, he timidly crossed the street to Prinsenhof. The pistols, loaded with poisonous bullets, were tucked in his girdle. His long coat concealed everything.

At Prinsenhof the guards saluted him. In the dimly lit foyer, he hid in a dark niche beside the stairs. Wild with desire, his heart pounded against his ribs. The sound of happy voices drifted to him from the dining hall. Suddenly the prince came out of the room. He was on his way to his workroom to sign the promised passport, for the messenger who would probably soon return.

William had reached the foot of the stairs when the wretch sprang from his hiding place firing both pistols. The prince collapsed. One of his friends gathered him up in his arms. William's sister rushed to the scene. His poor wife . . .

A deathly pallor had spread across the prince's face. Gently they lowered him to the floor. They heard his soft spoken words, "My God, my God, have pity on my soul and on this poor people!"

124

"This poor people!" He could hardly say those words, but the last words of this noble man had been a prayer to God for the people of the Netherlands for whom he had suffered and struggled and prayed so much. For them he had sacrificed everything — even his life.

The prince's sister, in a voice choked with tears, asked him, "Do you give your soul into the hands of the Lord Jesus?"

"Yes," he whispered faintly. With eyes full of compassion, he gazed at his beloved wife and died.

Balthasar Gerards, the villain, had escaped! Not past the guards, but across the small open place beside the house, along a narrow passage which ended at the garden wall, he ran. There was no one to stop him. He had provided himself with two pig bladders and a slender pipe to inflate them. Unable to swim, he knew he could use the bladders to keep afloat and so cross the canal. There a horse awaited him. But in his frenzied flight, he stumbled into a manure pile on the other side of the wall. A guard seized him and in heated fury beat him down.

Frightened people came running from all over. The quiet town was in an uproar.

"Dead! Was Father William dead?"

It was unbelievable! Tears flowed, and, in their sorrow and anger, they longed to tear apart that villainous wretch — that pious hypocrite who had murdered their beloved Prince. However, the soldiers stopped them and protected the murderer. The judge would pronounce judgment, not the people.

The fate of Balthasar Gerards was terrible. He was tortured, but the demented fanatic did not complain. Not a moan passed his lips. Proud of his deed, he never repented. The final verdict was the death penalty. The hand that had shot the fatal bullet was scorched with a red-hot iron. His dead body was quartered, his head severed. Those fierce and cruel eyes were now closed forever. The head was impaled on a pike and exhibited on the town wall of Delft. There was no one to help that wretched murderer, no one to speak up in his defense. The only person who could have interfered on his behalf had been forever silenced. Orange himself. Two years before, when the cashier Venero, and the monk Timmerman, accomplices of Jean Jauregui, had been executed, they had feared the torturing rack more than death itself. It was the custom of that time to precede death with many cruel forms of punishment. The Prince of Orange had saved those two from being tortured. From his sickbed the prince had sent a message to the judge, asking him to spare the guilty men from torture. Thus Venero and Timmerman had died quickly.

The people had regarded the prince's mercy as foolishness. Who could understand that generous, noble heart? Now that heart had stopped beating, and for Balthasar Gerards there would be no mercy. The blind fool had died in agony, yet he died proudly. He had done a great service for the holy Roman church. She had been delivered from her greatest enemy.

But William of Orange was not an enemy of the Roman church. He never had been. He, himself, had learned to serve his God in the Reformed church — the church of the Reformation. However, his whole life had been devoted to the struggle for freedom of conscience for everyone. He had never hated the Roman Catholic church. For Protestants and Roman Catholics alike, he had wanted to be their leader, the father of them all. The enmity between the two had always caused him grief. In revenge for what they often had to suffer themselves, the crude "beggars"[1] had at times treated the priests and monks cruelly. Often anyone who was Roman Catholic was a victim of their vengeance. But William of Orange could not be blamed for these actions. Whenever possible he had punished that cruelty. The people of that dark era had considered him to be much too tolerant, too compassionate, too indifferent. Often they had slandered him, reviled him, and reproached him for being a friend of the Roman Catholics.

Who could understand that noble, generous heart? Now he lay on his deathbed, white and cold. Thousands came to pay their final respects, to gaze at his kind and faithful face. They came to salute him, "Father of the Fatherland," one last time. Tears filled the eyes of many, and sorrow and compassion filled their hearts. They stood there as children who had lost their father. Great and deep was their grief, but greater and deeper was their love and reverence. He lay so quietly, so peacefully, as one who had fallen asleep after a long, difficult day of work. It seemed as though a smile lingered on his lips. He lay there a hero. He had finished his great and difficult task. God in heaven, who directs the lives of all people, had given rest to his faithful servant — eternal life in the glory of heaven.

Prince William was buried in the New Church in Delft. As an eminent prince, his body was carried by twelve noblemen. All other pomp and splendour was subdued. Thousands

---

[1] Protestants.

followed the sad procession. Children wept in the streets. Inside the church, beside the grave, the preacher Arend Cornelisz held a short oration. From the Bible, he read Revelation 14:13: "Blessed are the dead which die in the Lord from henceforth: Yea, saith the Spirit, that they may rest from their labours; and their works do follow them!"

\*       \*       \*

Philip of Spain, the real murderer, sneered, "I am the victor! Now who will stand by this stubborn people since he cannot help them anymore?"

Philip was a foolish tyrant. Had Orange's last prayer for "this poor people" been in vain? Who would help them now? But, more than ever before, the prayers rose to heaven. In the Netherlands, faith grew. "God will help!" More determined than ever, the people wanted to continue the fearsome struggle to the end. More clearly than before, they had learned the right way, shown to them by Orange himself. Risk everything, even life itself!

Yes, Philip, who did not deserve the title of "King," was a foolish king. Had he won? No. Rather he had lost everything, even though he did not know it yet. No one knew it. Philip had not seen a very sad boy walking behind the bier in Orange's funeral procession. Prince Maurice was seventeen years old. Philip had also not seen the tiny six-month-old baby, Prince Frederick Henry, sleeping in his cradle in quiet Prinsenhof. Philip had heartlessly murdered the father of both boys.

Be careful, King Philip. God rules and God is just!

Called by God, Prince William of Orange had laid the foundation for the house of freedom in the Netherlands. His task was finished. Prince Maurice would build the walls upon that foundation. Then one day, Prince Frederick Henry would complete the house. Philip with his power, craftiness, and wickedness would be stricken down. Throughout the ages his name would be cursed. Throughout the ages the name of William of Orange, "Father of the Fatherland," would be blessed.

*The marble tombstone at the New Church in Delft*

# 24. If . . .

If all the names of the great and good men of the beautiful history of the Netherlands were written in a list, whose name would be first? Would it be the name of the one who had conquered in battle or of the one who had discovered new lands, winning them for his homeland? Or would it perhaps be the name of one who had made the country rich and famous or who had been feared and honoured by the rest of the world? Certainly, the names of all of these, and many more wise and faithful men, would be written on that list. But at the top would shine the name of William of Orange, the man who had never considered his own welfare. He who became poor with the oppressed; he who had been despised and reviled, slandered and threatened; the hero who never held back, not even from the most difficult sacrifice. He who had given his all, even his life — his name would be in the place of honour.

\*　　\*　　\*

If William of Orange would have remained a prince at Dillenburg, then he would have been forgotten, just as most other princes and dukes have been. If William of Orange had remained Philip's faithful servant or had fallen for the riches and honour offered so enticingly, then he would have been forgotten, just as so many of Philip's henchmen have been. Then who would have been the one to involve himself in the affairs of the people of the Netherlands during those dark and anxious days, enduring distress, suffering, and death. Only he could have done that great work, not in his own strength, but because he had known himself to have been called by God.

Moses, the wealthy prince in Pharaoh's household, had been chosen by God to deliver his people from Egyptian slavery. He had endured poverty and suffering, as well as sorrow and distress inflicted by his own people. Moses, himself, never lived in the promised land.

William, the wealthy prince in Philip's court, was chosen by God to deliver his people in the Netherlands from the Spanish tyranny. He had endured poverty, suffering, and death. Often his own people did not understand him, and, often, they failed to appreciate him. William never saw the freedom of his beloved country.

Without Orange there may not have been Netherlanders. Perhaps, during the course of time, they would have become French or German. That tiny country on the sea would have become a province of one or another greater empire. But God had given them the Prince of Orange, and they have been allowed to become a small, brave, nation in their own beautiful country.

\*　　　\*　　　\*

If someone would now say, But that all happened so long ago, almost four hundred years ago, what remains now? What would we answer? We could say, Prinsenhof still stands in Delft with its dark stairway, and the bullet holes from the murderers' pistols are still in the wall. The beautiful tomb in the New Church, with the faithful little dog at the prince's feet, still exists. A beautiful statue of a horse and rider stands before the royal palace in The Hague.

But if that were all we could say, it would be better to remain silent. Then what really remains? There is something of far greater value than an old house with bullet holes, a tomb, and a statue. It is the beautiful heritage of Reformed believers all over the world. The love and gratitude for that fearless and blameless knight still remains. That is a thousand times more valuable than a grave, or bullet holes, or a statue. Who would not think of Orange with utmost respect? He had given himself to his people. His people had given themselves to him. For all time, these two are united. It was God's will. The Netherlands and Orange belonged together.

Prince Maurice followed in the footsteps of his father, and then William's younger son, Frederick Henry, took over. Then followed William II and William III and all the other members of the House of Orange throughout history. They had all been loyal to their people, and the people had been loyal to them. It had been God's will that the Netherlands and the House of Orange were to be united.

Today the Dutch queen, William's descendant, reigns. William and his little group of people, threatened and oppressed, together have followed the way set out by God. That was the beginning of the Dutch history. The way has been dangerous and difficult, but God has given His blessing.

Today, Queen Juliana[1], who bears the name of her great grandmother, the mother of William, as a beautiful remembrance of that noble woman, and the strong, free people who have remained loyal to her, are following the same path through history with courage and trust as Prince William. This also is God's will. Our time is also filled with danger and difficulty, but God has given His blessing. If someone would ask, What remains of that old, distant, forgotten, time hundreds of years ago? Then we would say, The Netherlands and Orange are still one in love and faithfulness. This is what remains: a legacy of great value, a gift of God.

If William, Prince of Orange would return now, he would look around in amazement with joy and gratitude in his heart. Today the skies are not darkened with the horrible smoke

---

[1] Queen Juliana was Queen of the Netherlands from 1948-1980. The author wrote this book in 1933 when Queen Wilhelmina ruled in the Netherlands, but in later editions he mentioned Queen Juliana. Since 1980 Queen Beatrix rules in the Netherlands.

of the burning stakes, and no one is tortured or murdered for serving God in the manner he feels is right. Soldiers no longer tramp through the countryside, burning and looting greedily.

Orange would think, Oh blessed country, how my heart had always longed for such peace and tranquillity for you!

He would see many beautiful churches, for Protestants as well as for Roman Catholics and Jews. His heart would warm at the total freedom of religion that exists, and he would shout, "This is what I have always desired!"

But he would also feel disappointed. He would see that, in our time, many people never go to church, never read the Bible, are indifferent, and no longer serve God. Oh, he would be filled with an overwhelming sadness. "Have my faithful people suffered so much, even death, for this?"

Today no one speaks about Spain, but the name of Orange is on many lips. After more than four hundred years, Prince William, "Father of the Fatherland," has not been forgotten. He would be pleased. He would see that after such a long time one of his descendants of the renowned House of Orange, Queen Wilhelmina, had continued and persevered in the same faith in God as he had during the darkest hour of the history of his people. In 1940 she was forced to flee her beloved country to escape from a foreign tyrant. But in exile she also remained caring and trusting through sorrow and anxiety. In this she has honoured the name of her famous forefather. Prince William would also see Juliana, Prince Bernhard, and the princesses; his heart would be filled with joy. He would think, Juliana! She bears the name of my beloved and devout mother. Oh may she be just like her!

He would realize that also today life is difficult, full of worries, full of threats and dangers. Who knows what the future will bring? This would make him sad, but he would give reassurance, saying, "My life was also difficult, but I followed, by the grace of God, the course set out by Him for me. Take courage, do what is right as befits a member of the family of Orange. Be faithful unto the end."

Again he would be hearing the familiar lines of the song written by his good friend, Marnix of St. Aldegonde, the song that has lived on.

*William of Nassau, scion*
*Sprung of an ancient line,*
*I dedicate . . .*

His heart would jump for joy. They have not forgotten me! Neither have they forgotten the martyrs and the exiles or my faithful beggars. Even my people of Briele and Alkmaar, of Haarlem and Leyden, are honoured by the people of today!

If he really could come back, Prince William's head would bow in prayer. Through suffering and death, my people have been delivered by Thee, O my God! Let them not forsake Thee, Thou Who directeth the lives of all people. May they never be proud in their own strength, but be strong through faith. Wilt Thou, heavenly Father, never forsake Thy people!

*Their shield and their reliance,*
*O God, Thou ever wert.*
*They trust unto Thy guidance.*
*O leave them not ungirt.*

## Het Wilhelmus - Dutch version

Wilhelmus van Nassouwe
Ben ik van Duitsen bloed.
Den vaderland getrouwe
Blijf ik tot in den doet.
Een prinse van Oranje
Ben ik vrij onverveerd.
De koning van Hispanje
Heb ik altijd geeerd.

In Godes vrees te leven
Heb ik altijd betracht.
Daarom ben ik verdreven,
Om land, om luid gebracht.
Maar God zal mij regeren
Als een goed instrument,
Dat ik zal wederkeren
In mijnen regiment.

Lijdt u, mijn onderzaten,
Die oprecht zijn van aard.
God zal u niet verlaten,
Al zijt gij nu bezwaard.
Die vroom begeert te leven,
Bidt God nacht ende dag,
Dat Hij mij kracht wil geven,
Dat ik u helpen mag.

Lijf en goed altesamen
Heb ik u niet verschoond.
Mijn broeders, hoog van namen,
Hebben 't u ook vertoond:
Graaf Adolf is gebleven
In Friesland, in de slag.
Zijn ziel in 't eeuwig leven
Verwacht de jongste dag.

Edel en hooggeboren
Van keizerlijke stam,
Een vorst des rijks verkoren,
Als een vroom christen-man,
Voor Godes woord geprezen
Heb ik vrij onversaagd,
Als een held zonder vrezen,
Mijn edel bloed gewaagd.

Mijn schild ende betrouwen
Zijt Gij, o God, mijn Heer.
Op U zo wil ik bouwen.
Verlaat mij nimmermeer:
Dat ik doch vroom mag blijven,
Uw dienaar t'aller stond,
De tirannie verdrijven,
Die mij mijn hert doorwondt.

Van al die mij bezwaren
En mijn vervolgers zijn,
Mijn God, wil doch bewaren
De trouwe dienaar Dijn:
Dat zij mij niet verrassen
In hare boze moed,
Haar handen niet en wassen
In mijn onschuldig bloed.

Als David moeste vluchten
Voor Saul, de tiran,
Zo heb ik moeten zuchten
Met menig eldelman.
Maar God heeft hem verheven,
Verlost uit alle nood,
Een koninkrijk gegeven
In Israel zeer groot.

Na 't zuur zal ik ontvangen
Van God mijn Heer dat zoet.
Daarnaar zo doet verlangen
Mijn vorstelijk gemoed,
Dat is, dat ik mag sterven
Met ere in het veld,
Een eeuwig rijk verwerven
Als een getrouwe held.

Niets doet mij meer erbarmen
In mijne wederspoed,
Dan dat men ziet verarmen
Des konings landen goed.
Dat u de Spanjaards krenken,
O edel Neerland zoet,
Als ik daaraan gedenke,
Mijn edel hert dat bloedt.

Als een prins opgezeten
Met mijner heires kracht,
Van de tiran vermeten
Heb ik de slag verwacht.
Die bij Maastricht begraven,
Bevreesde mijn geweld.
Mijn ruiters zag men draven
Zeer moedig door het veld.

Soo het de wil des Heren
Op die tijd was geweest,
Had ik geern willen keren
Van u dit zwaar tempeest:
Maar de Heer van hierboven,
Die alle ding regeert,
Die men altijd moet loven,
En heeft het niet begeerd.

Seer christ'lijk was gedreven
Mijn prinselijk gemoed.
Standvastig is gebleven
Mijn hert in tegenspoed.
De Heer heb ik gebeden
Van mijnes herten grond,
Dat Hij mijn zaak wil reden,
Mijn onschuld doen bekond.

Oorlof, mijn arme schapen,
Die zijt in grote nood,
Uw Herder zal niet slapen,
Al zijt gij nu verstrooit:
Tot God wilt u begeven,
Zijn heilzaam woord neemt aan.
Als vrome Christ'nen leven;
't Zal hier haast zijn gedaan.

Voor God wil ik belijden
En Zijner groten macht,
Dat ik tot genen tijden
De koning heb veracht:
Maar dat ik God de Here,
Der Hoogster Majesteit,
Heb moeten obedieren
In der gerechtigheid.

The first letters of each stanza form the name

**WILLEM VAN NASSOV**

## Wilhelmus - English version

William of Nassau, scion
Sprung of an ancient line,
I dedicate undying
Faith to this land of mine.
A prince I am, undaunted,
Of Orange, ever free.
The king of Spain I've granted
My lifelong loyalty.

I've ever tried to live in
The fear of God's command,
And therefore I've been driven
From people, home, and land.
But God, I trust, will rate me
His willing instrument
And one day reinstate me
Into my government.

Let no despair betray you,
My subjects true and good.
The Lord will surely stay you
Though now you are pursued.
He who would live devoutly
Must pray God day and night
To throw his power about me
As champion of your right.

Life and my all for others
I sacrificed, for you!
And my illustrious brothers
Proved their devotion too.
Count Adolf, more's the pity,
Fell in the Frisian fray,
And in the eternal city
Awaits the judgment day.

I, nobly born, descended
From an imperial stock,
An Empire's prince, defended
(Braving the battle's shock
Heroically and fearless
As pious Christians ought)
With my life's blood the peerless
Gospel of God our Lord.

A shield and my reliance,
O God, Thou ever wert,
I'll trust unto Thy guidance.
O leave me not ungirt,
That I may stay a pious
Servant of Thine for aye,
And drive the plagues that try us
And tyranny away.

My God, I pray Thee, save me
For all who do pursue
And threaten to enslave me,
Thy trusted servant true.
O Father, do not sanction
Their wicked, foul design;
Let them not wash their hands in
This guiltless blood of mine.

Once David searched for shelter
From King Saul's tyranny.
E'en so I fled this welter
And many a lord with me.
But God the Lord did save him
From exile and its hell
And, in His mercy, gave him
A realm in Israel.

Fear not 't will rain sans ceasing;
The clouds are bound to part.
I bide the sight so pleasing
Unto my princely heart:
That when I death encounter
I honour find therein
And as a faithful warrior
The eternal realm may win.

No thing so moves my pity
As seeing through these lands
Field, village, town, and city
Pillaged by roving bands.
O that the Spaniards rape thee,
My Netherlands so sweet —
The thought of that does grip me,
Causing my heart to bleed.

A stride on steed of mettle
I've waited with my host
The tyrant's call to battle,
Who durst not do his boast.
For, near Maestricht, in hiding,
He feared the force I wield:
My horsemen were seen riding
Bravely across the field.

Surely, if God had willed it,
When that fierce tempest blew,
My power would have stilled it,
Or turned its blast from you.
But He Who dwells in heaven,
Whence all our blessings flow,
For which aye praise be given,
**Did not desire it so.**

Steadfast my heart remaineth
In my adversity.
My princely courage straineth
All nerves to live and be.
I've prayed the Lord my Master
With fervid heart and tense
To save me from disaster
And prove my innocence.

Alas, my flock! To sever
Is hard on us. Farewell.
Your Shepherd wakes, wherever
Dispersed you may dwell.
Pray God that He may ease you;
His Gospel be your cure.
Walk in the steps of Jesu.
This life will not endure.

Unto God and His power
I do confession make
That ne'er at any hour
Ill of the king I spake.
But to the Lord, the greatest
Of majesties, I owe
Obedience first and latest,
For Justice wills it so.

The first letters of each stanza form the name

WILLIAM OF NASSAU

# WHAT IS THE ADVANTAGE OF BECOMING A MEMBER
## OF THE *INHERITANCE BOOK CLUB?*

* As a member you will get the new books of Inheritance Publications at a special price (usually at about 15 % discount) sent to you within about thirty days after publication.
* You have the right to return new I.P. books within 10 days from the day of delivery.
* You don't have to send an order each time a new book is published.
* Members can obtain at any time any number of current I.P. or Premier books at the original special Publication Price, unless the book has been out of print.
* There is no postage charge!

**You can join different categories.**

Cat. A: Selected new books from Inheritance Publications (about 5 books per year)
Cat. B: Selected new children- and adult-fiction books from I.P. (about 3 books per year)
Cat. C: Selected new study books from I.P. (about 2 books per year)
Cat. D: Selected new books from I.P. and Premier Publishing (about 7 books per year)
Cat. E: Selected new study books from I.P. and Premier Publishing (about 5 books per year)
Inheritance Publications reserves the right to terminate a membership.
Our books are usually based on historical facts or contain sound biblical doctrines.

**Titles that are currently available at special prices to I.P. Members:**

|  | reg.price | I.P.member price |  |
|---|---|---|---|
| PIET PRINS - SHADOW 4 - THE PARTISANS | CN.$ 7.95 | CN.$ 6.75 | U.S.$ 5.95 |
| PIET PRINS - SHADOW 5 - SABOTAGE | CN.$ 7.95 | CN.$ 6.75 | U.S.$ 5.95 |
| PIET PRINS - ANAK, THE ESKIMO BOY | CN.$ 6.95 | CN.$ 5.95 | U.S.$ 4.95 |
| PIET PRINS - WHEN THE MORNING CAME (STRUGGLE FREEDOM 1) | CN.$ 9.95 | CN.$ 8.50 | U.S.$ 7.50 |
| J.A. KNEPPER SR. - WHOLESOME COMMUNICATION | CN.$ 9.95 | CN.$ 8.50 | U.S.$ 7.50 |
| J. FABER - ESSAYS IN REFORMED DOCTRINE | CN.$19.95 | CN.$16.95 | U.S.$14.95 |
| C. VAN DER WAAL - THE COVENANTAL GOSPEL | CN.$17.95 | CN.$15.50 | U.S.$13.50 |
| L. ERKELENS - THE CROWN OF HONOUR | CN.$11.95 | CN.$ 9.95 | U.S.$ 9.25 |
| RUDOLF VAN REEST - SCHILDER'S STRUGGLE FOR UNITY/CHURCH | CN.$29.95 | CN.$25.50 | U.S.$22.50 |
| P.K. KEIZER - CHURCH HISTORY | CN.$12.95 | CN.$10.95 | U.S.$ 9.95 |
| T. PLANTINGA - CHRISTIAN PHILOSOPHY WITHIN BIBL. BOUNDS | CN.$ 7.95 | CN.$ 6.95 | U.S.$ 5.95 |
| N.D. KLOOSTERMAN - THE RELATION BETWEEN CHR. LIBERTY | CN.$11.95 | CN.$ 9.95 | U.S.$ 9.25 |
| CLARENCE STAM - LIVING IN THE JOY OF FAITH | CN.$39.95 | CN.$31.95 | U.S.$22.50 |
| J. VAN BRUGGEN - ANNOTATIONS TO THE HEIDELBERG CATECHISM | CN.$15.95 | CN.$13.50 | U.S.$30.50 |
| C. VANDERWAAL - HAL LINDSEY AND BIBLICAL PROPHECY | CN.$ 9.95 | CN.$ 8.50 | U.S.$ 7.50 |
| RUDOLF VAN REEST - ISRAEL'S HOPE AND EXPECTATION | CN.$19.95 | CN.$16.95 | U.S.$14.95 |
| AN ROOK - JUDY'S OWN PET KITTEN | CN.$ 4.95 | CN.$ 3.95 | U.S.$ 3.60 |
| WILLIAM P. BALKENENDE - LOVE IN TIMES OF REFORMATION | CN.$ 8.95 | CN.$ 7.60 | U.S.$ 6.60 |

# INHERITANCE BOOK CLUB MEMBERSHIP FORM

Name _____ Date _____

Address _____

City & Province _____

Postal code _____ Tel. _____

Membership Category _____ Signature _____

Please complete the membership form and return it to:
**Inheritance Publications  Box 154, Neerlandia, Alberta T0G 1R0  Canada**